User-Designed
Computing

Lexington Books Series in Computer Science

Kenneth J. Thurber, General Editor

User-Designed Computing

Free-Enterprise
Application Design

Louis Schlueter, Jr.
Sperry Univac

LexingtonBooks
D.C. Heath and Company
Lexington, Massachusetts
Toronto

Library of Congress Cataloging in Publication Data

Schlueter, Louis
    User-designed computing.

    Includes index.
    1. System design. 2. Interactive computer systems. I. Title.
QA76.9.S88S34   001.64   81-48511
ISBN 0-669-05377-5   AACR2

FASTRAND, SPERRY UNIVAC, UNISCOPE, UNISERVO, Speristar, and
UNIVAC are registered trademarks of the Sperry Corporation. MAPPER and
PAGEWRITER are additional trademarks of the Sperry Corporation.

Published simultaneously in Canada

Printed in the United States of America

International Standard Book Number: 0-669-05377-5

Library of Congress Catalog Card Number: 81-48511

Contents

Contents   vii

Figures and Tables

Figures

Tables

Preface

The power of computer technology is awesome. Fantastic technological breakthroughs have been made in microcircuitry, minicomputerization, hardware and memory designs, even computer-designed computers. Computer power is cheap and abundantly available. Each new computer family brings exponential performance improvement. The comparison has been made that, had the automobile industry made comparable strides in performance improvement, we could be driving the equivalent of a Mercedes for about $200. The remarkable fact about all this multiplication of computer power is that the magnitudes of performance improvement of the past decade will surely be repeated during the next decade. Not only is tremendous computing power already available but it will be many times greater and cheaper in the future. There is no energy crisis here.

The development of computer power has been a relatively silent revolution. Its dimensions are clearly known only to perceptive industry technicians. Those people not associated with the computing industry are almost unaware that this extremely important revolution continues to occur. Computer technology is a world of cuneiform hieroglyphics as far as they are concerned. They know that masses of data are being processed by computers, but they do not think of it as information. In this world they need information—timely, up-to-the-minute information—to control their daily endeavors.

Most people today process this information on paper, with forms and copiers. They also make many telephone calls and person-to-person communications. This is an inefficient way to process information. If they could computerize this daily information flow, they would be at least ten times more efficient. Think of this: if the paper processors of our work force could be ten times more efficient in processing information, what a tremendous productivity improvement would be achieved. What a productive, vibrant economy we would have!

The challenge then is to provide a means of computerizing these hundreds of millions of paper mills and inefficient communications. The difficulty is that, individually, these volatile sets of information exchanges are not significant enough to justify computerization with conventional programming methods. Each is quite unique. Just creating the specifications needed to define all these individual programs would be an impossible task, not to mention the armies of programmers and enormous amounts of computer time and effort needed to code, compile, and debug all these programs. And, even if all these programs were written, they would quickly become obsolete because of changing requirements, the only dependable factor in all this information flow.

Fortunately, it is possible to computerize all this manually implemented information flow. It can be done by providing a *user-oriented* or, as the industry now calls it, a *user-friendly* computer language that allows end-users to be architects of their own systems and directors of computer power. But more than an easy language is needed in this approach to information processing. A service environment must be provided with many of the same elements of the free-enterprise system that has made this country a success. Only with end-user freedom to apply computer power can the full benefits be obtained. Only with user-operational knowledge and innovative talent unfettered by the bureaucracies of the data-processing establishments can all the needed applications be established and kept current.

Creating a computer system that can support a Free Enterprise Computing environment is not a problem. The whole computer industry is tending toward the development of user-oriented, user-friendly computer systems. One of the finest of this type of system exists and is provided in the kind of system that is generically termed a *report-processing system*. The challenge lies in effectively applying these user-oriented systems in such a way as to create and preserve a free-enterprise environment for the end-user. Part of the problem in this lies in the fact that the data-processing establishment has seldom given computing freedom to the end-user. They have been the providers and controllers of almost all computer power. It is often unfamiliar and threatening for many data-processing personnel to even consider concepts of freedom for end-users.

For highly experienced data-processing personnel, it is often inconceivable that directing computers can be simple enough for users to do. It is unthinkable to let an end-user build his or her own system and directly control computer power. Yet it is under the auspices of the existing data-processing organizations that the Free Enterprise Computing system environment must be created—a challenge indeed given the prevailing disciplinary orientation of such organizations. An environment of freedom for people as well as computer users is a simple yet fragile thing that can be seriously damaged by overcontrol.

This book will examine the term *real-time information* and distinguish this as *real-control information*. It will examine the problems inherent in conventional computer-program specification and design. The problem of computerizing real-control information will be addessed as well as the resolution of this problem inherent in the concept of making the end-user the architect of his or her own systems. The implications of this approach will be examined as it affects system purchase, application specification and development, system design, and productive use.

New management attitudes and philosophies must be understood and fostered to bring free enterprise to the use of computing power. This book will explain how data-processing management can deliver large-scale, user-oriented computer services and yet effectively manage the related computer resources and provide system safety. Guidance will be provided for user management that can be used to ensure that the user's operation is able to obtain direct access to computer power with all the potential for productivity improvement that such access implies. The goal then is "Free Enterprise Computing." It is a worthy goal capable of having equally catalytic effects on information processing as free enterprise has had on existing economic systems.

Acknowledgments

Portions of this book are based on material copyrighted by Sperry Corporation and are used with permission of Sperry Corporation. The concepts, perceptions, and opinions expressed in this book are not necessarily those of Sperry Univac.

A summary dissertation on the concepts of Free Enterprise Computing were presented in *UNISPHERE Magazine,* September 1981, in the article "MAPPER: A Comprehensive Overview, Part I," portions of which are reprinted here with permission of UNISPHERE Publishing Company, P.O. Box 38085, Dallas, Texas 75238.

This book is dedicated to the developers and supporters of Report Processing System concepts at Sperry Univac®, a division of the Sperry Corporation. Their years of consistent pursuit of excellence in system design and implementation have established an example that undeniably proves the viability and value of the concepts of Free Enterprise Computing. It is also dedicated to the memory of Doran L. Edinger for his many contributions to the cause.

**User-Designed
Computing**

1 Computer Programming and Users

The electronic-data-processing power of computers is awesome. Millions of logical computations can be performed in just seconds. In recent years we have seen the millisecond, microsecond, nanosecond, and now picasecond computer instruction become realities in computer technology. Not too many years ago the speed of light, at which electricity travels, was thought to be a significant limitation to computer-processing speeds. It takes some fraction of time for current to flow through the interconnecting wires of the computers. Then circuit patterns were photoreduced to create microcircuitry, which then made the distance among logic elements microscopic and simultaneously improved mass production of circuitry manufacture. Resistance to current flow is now being eliminated with the introduction of circuitry operating in resistance-free environments. Computer performance and capability have thus improved dramatically in the past decades and they should continue to grow in the future.

The drawback in current computer technology is the fact that all digital computers rely exclusively on yes and no logical decisions, albeit performed with electronic speed. Thus computers are "fast and stupid." In other words, computers are powerful information processors, but they perform only as disciplined by the art of programming.

The disciplining of computers, *programming*, has evolved into a multibillion-dollar industry. However, there are few end-users (those who must apply information from computers) who are comfortable or even satisfied in their dealings with programmers and programming establishments. Communicating with the programmer is often a source of great frustration and expense for the end-user. The user more often than not finds his or her needs to be of too low a priority to be computerized. If the need is great enough to warrant the cost of designing the program, the user encounters other difficulties. The demand for programmer talent is intense. Actual program design and debugging, once started, take many months or even many years to complete.

The problem of communicating with the programmers is worse than the problems of costs and delays. Defining the task for the computer to accomplish is the greatest problem. However, the key to that problem is the programmer's ability to think about the task definition as if he or she were the end-user. Therein lies the crux of the problem: the art of computer programming is technically complex and syntactically confusing to the layman,

1

and the operational world of the end-user is equally complex and confusing to the computer technician. So the tasks to be programmed must be carefully defined, usually with a written, detailed specification. Needless to say, much is missed or confused in the process. The result is great expense, delays, confusion, and programs that do not suit the ideal operational environment. The very best the user can get is what the programmer *thinks* the user wants or what the programmer *thinks* the user needs.

When programs are made operational, user management soon discovers that the implementation of new management policies must take into account the costs and delays in reprogramming. Sometimes extensive programmed systems calcify and even direct corporate policy instead of remaining passively utilitarian. Indeed, considering all the costs, delays, frustrations, and communication problems in the programming discipline, it is not surprising that so little of the total business or institutional information-processing requirement is computerized.

Energy sources have been cited as a limiting factor to our economy. But the programming bottleneck may be an even greater limiting factor. Vast amounts of computer power are already available at reasonable costs, and computer power will be even more abundant and cheaper in the future. Effective use of this enormous power could unleash fantastic productivity in all our industry, institution, and government operations. But even with current levels of computer use, severe shortages of programmer resources exist. It is essential that this resource crisis be overcome so that the power inherent in our current and future computer technologies can be effectively harnessed. Thus computer systems must be capable of being directly adapted to information-processing applications without programming intermediaries.

The computer industry is in a situation similar to that faced by the telephone industry years ago when telephone-call connections were made manually with plugs by telephone operators. An assessment was made at that time by the telephone company of the potential growth in the volume of telephone calls to be made in the future. It was obvious that the armies of telephone operators that would be needed to match the demand for telephone service created an unacceptable limitation to the telephone service of the future. So the phone company's solution to the problem was to automate and computerize the switching mechanisms and to place in the end-user's hands the ability to direct this switching. The result was the dial telephone. When the customer dials a number, he or she directs the computer power of the telephone system. The customer is then the operator. And by placing the power to direct their switching computers in the customers' hands, the telephone operator bottleneck was overcome.

A similar situation exists in the computing industry today. A tremendous need exists to computerize the flow of *real-control information*. Data-processing staffs are burdened with maintenance of the existing structured systems. They face large backlogs of service requests for new programs, and adequate personnel can neither be hired nor trained fast enough to meet the demand. Thus there exists a trend toward user-oriented computer systems. Again, placing in the hands of the end-users the ability to direct computer power is a giant step forward in meeting the demand for computer technology. *Free-enterprise report processing*, the subject of this book, makes accessible to end-users that which is impossible with structured designer approaches. The user-oriented age of computers arrives. Free-enterprise computing becomes a reality.

2 Real-Time Information

The definition of what constitutes *real-time information* is highly debatable. Computer technicians tend to use finite specifications like "average seconds of response time for a processing query," and they suggest that any transaction that has more than a 4-second average response time cannot be considered real-time. Systems are actually compared in that manner.

Perhaps a better term than "real-time information" is "real-control information." The definition of *real-control information* allows varying availability time factors to be measured in terms of control effectiveness. In other words, if the information can be accessed conveniently and in time so that it can be used to affect the control of events, it can be considered real-control information. Conversely then, if data is not accessible in time to control events, it is reference data. It is suitable only to evaluate patterns of event occurrences after they have transpired. Reference data can influence upcoming events only if such data shows evidence of repeating patterns.

The real-control information needed in most work situations is primarily that which pertains to:

1. *Transactions about to enter the operation.* Information about these transactions is needed to prepare the resources to handle them and to schedule them in conjunction with other transactions.
2. *Transactions in the operation.* Information about these transactions is needed for tracking purposes to ensure movement through the operation. Status reporting, exception reporting, and expediting are all key activities in this control.
3. *Transactions that just left the operation.* This recent history needs accessibility for the immediate follow-up, that is, when did it finish, what were the cost factors and shipping information, and so on.

This information usually does not amount to a large amount of data. Most people do not actually work with large amounts of data. The mind processes small sets of information, not volumes. A great concern is that of setting priorities and of expediting tasks using this dynamic set of useful information as the basis of decision and action. The information is really useful only when it is available on a timely basis and is in a format that exactly suits the method and environment of the operation in the specific office or work area where it is used.

Real-control information can be considered as data viewed through a "window of time." Thus time is the important factor; that is, the information that is needed to control the present operation. This is the type of control that is now exercised in the millions of manual paper mills that make up modern offices. The control is very ineffective, and the manual processing is very inefficient.

Once the information has passed through this "window of time," it becomes data, reference data. In the manual paper mills, it is then stored in file cabinets or on microfiche or, in a few cases—"few" relative to the total flow of real-control information—it is fed into computers. Prevailing computer technology is good at storing and processing large amounts of data.

**Real-Time Information Processing
without Computers**

It is remarkable that today's entire business-government-institutional world has no practical computer capabilities to employ in the true, real-time information processing that constitutes the daily set of tasks and actions. In most offices the information processing involved in this minute-to-minute work is manually performed with papers, forms, ledgers, log books, and card files (that never see a computer) and notes of every conceivable type. These manually manipulated paper media provide the real-time information (not data) that most people in most offices use to make their minute-to-minute decisions, plan their priorities, and perform their daily tasks. This up-to-the-minute information processing cannot wait for keypunching and the twenty-four-hour batch service. For the most part, it is performed manually and therefore very inefficiently.

This manual paper shuffling is the predominant operational characteristic in most offices of large corporations as well as small companies. Indeed, the smaller the company, the less the use of computer technology. The vast number of small businesses, who generate the greater part of our national economy and employ most of the work force, do not use computers. The under $10-million-gross business with any significant computerization of its real-time information flow is so scarce that it is statistically insignificant in the overall computer industry. Only the large, common clerical functions have been given a type of "real-time," transactional computer service. Examples of these would be airline-reservations systems and insurance-claims processing. The uncommon real-time control information that constitutes the vast majority of operational management information remains uncomputerized.

In the relatively few offices that have access to computer services, the usual service provided is that of the batch-processed payroll, and accounts-receivable computer-print listing. This is data. It is reference data, not control information. Such listings usually consist of data in excess of 10,000 lines (or it would not be worth computer processing). The data in such listings is usually a week old (state-of-the-art printouts contain yesterday's data!). The high-speed-printing capabilities of modern computer systems are too often used to provide too much data, rather than the needed data organized in a practical format.

Computerizing Real-Control Information

Real-control information is the most difficult type of application to computerize. In fact, the majority of programmers in the industry are not skilled enough to do *real-time application programming*. Instantaneous-response times given to numerous simultaneous users of the same program is the essence of such computerization. To provide fast response while simultaneous access is occurring, these criteria must be characteristic of the successful real-time program used:

The program must be written in Assembler language. The inefficiencies of high-level languages such as COBOL or Fortran cannot be tolerated, and the inefficiencies of these languages would introduce unacceptable delays in processing. Only the "tightest and most elegant" Assembler code is effective enough to support the intense environment.

There must be an efficient communications-control routine. Control software for communication networks could be properly produced only by experienced communication programmers. The protocols and methodologies of the communication networks are complex and extremely sophisticated. Key to this programming is processing the variety of valid as well as erroneous conditions that can be presented on the communication lines.

There must be a low-overhead supervisor. Efficient control of the resources of the system implies a fast-response supervisor routine. Maintaining fast response in a resource-shared environment requires sophisticated element-cycling procedures and prompt conflict resolution.

Multipath processing must be part of the system. The *worker programs* (functions) must be capable of supporting numerous concurrent jobs of the same type with a single set of code in memory. This is called *reentrant programming*. With multiple, simultaneous jobs executing in the same code, sophisticated logic is required as well as a keen mind to extract the errors in the related, convoluted bomb dumps.

Relocatable element loading must be part of the system. The programs must be written to enable loading and executing from any area of memory. This is essential in sustaining a flow and blend in memory-resource utilization and to minimize and resolve memory deadlocks.

There must be a real-time data-base management system. Simultaneous, high-volume, real-time data-base updating must be supported. In other words, the program must support the resolution of not only tricky update conflicts but also the allowance of retrieval transactions while the base is being updated. An additional requirement in this data-base management is the design of fast-reliable recovery and history-production processes.

Programmers who can handle real-control system design are extremely hard to find, develop, or hold on to. Even when such programmers can be found, the system-design work is so complex and time consuming that the cost is prohibitive. And, finally, debugging these systems is the ultimate challenge since a random-access, real-time-use environment is impossible to debug with simulators. Given these considerations, it is no wonder that so little real-control information has been computerized.

3

Program Specifications

The preparation of the program specifications for conventional application design is a costly, complex, time-consuming task. However, it is essential because it is the means of conveying the idea from the user's conception to the programmer's mind so that the solution can be defined in the language of the computer. In the end, the specification also becomes a form of documentation for the program.

Program-specification preparation is essentially a science in itself. This is attested to by the fact that generally the user does not explain the requirement directly to the programmer; instead, he or she must communicate through one or more interpreters, who have various titles such as planner, systems analyst, specification writer, and documentation analyst. Sometimes, with the more complex applications, each of these functions will be applied by different individuals in a whole hierarchy of interpretation and qualification. With management review, analysis, and approval, the process is usually lengthy and very costly.

This expense is all justified on the basis that a clear definition of the application to be designed is essential so group thinking and committee design is introduced to bring a maximum of experience to the consideration of the problem. The goal is that by this juggling and multifaceted viewing, every aspect of the application requirement will be uncovered, identified, and documented. The reason this thoroughness is essential is that the application will be what is termed a *structured application*. In other words, the application will not be openended but will be designed to answer only the questions spelled out in the specification with clearly indicated logic and following a prescribed path or paths to the data base. The answers to be provided must likewise be specifically defined as to their presented form as well as the discrete logic by which they will be derived.

Communication is what specifying is intended to accomplish, communication between the user and the programmer code. Just as communication is probably the biggest problem in the world in general, it is a very large problem in the discipline of programming too. The mental image of the requirement as conceived by the user must be conveyed in oral or written form to the planner/system analyst. This first link is probably the weakest in the whole chain. Even the user who can effectively describe and communicate in written or oral form may have a concept of the requirement that is incomplete. The novice requestor is especially prone to poor problem definition due to a lack of knowledge of using computer resources.

The methodology of the development of program specifications is the subject of numerous books and seminars and is the basis of many consulting careers. Whole systems of specification development have been devised, promoted, and established, and all aim at making the presentation of the end requirement of the application as all encompassing as possible.

Dilemmas develop from the use of the predefined program specification. One is the fact that all aspects of the real requirement cannot be seen until the system is in use. Only from actual use can the realities of the requirement be determined. In use, the answers expose new questions.

Another problem with extensive, predefined program specification is that the documentary burden becomes a detriment to flexibility in actual system design. When appliction design is well along, a whole new approach or dimension to the application may become visible but will be ignored because modification of the voluminous specification would be too tedious. Specification development and modification can be a significant burden in itself. This is especially true where an extensive bureaucracy of specification approval exists. Serious calcification of an innovative programmer environment can be caused by a program-specification bureaucracy that is too rigid and pervasive.

The specifications and the system grow larger as the systems expand in use and scope. This only causes the problem of adaptation to be more and more difficult. Response time to new requirements becomes longer and longer. The systems grow because they are structured for specific logic. Each question to be answered and its input and output requirements and solution logic must be coded into the system structure, and each solution exposes new questions.

The coded program logic for the multitudes of problem solutions and all the specifications and documentation associated with all this system design are having their calcifying effects, not to mention the sheer complexity of the code itself. Industry studies show that 75 percent of data-processing efforts are now spent in maintaining existing systems. Is it any wonder that such dissatisfaction with data-processing performance exists through the industry today? We have had many years of system development now, and it is becoming apparent that serious levels of system calcification are being attained. It is said that "the last act of a dying organization is to write an all encompassing rule book." Perhaps the advanced state of the art of specification development is symptomatic of the "big rule book" in data processing.

4 Report-Processing Systems

The finest user-oriented computer-information systems available today are those generically described as *report-processing systems* (see chapter 18). These are powerful real-time, display-oriented information-processing systems. Used properly, they are capable of creating an ideal Free Enterprise computer-service environment. The concept of "report processing" has been in development and use for over ten years. It makes use of an extensive function list that the user can select from, as needed, in performing his real-time report processing. The systems also provide powerful inter faces to batch and demand processing as well as other systems. Many powerful tools are available for system use and resource management. A role of "report-processing systems coordinator" creates a key means of control for this service, which enables application planning and assurance of performance to plan.

Some of the existing report-processing systems have successfully established large and very effective real-time reporting environments that contain all the elements of a Free Enterprise computing service. However, some of these existing systems have fallen far short of their full potential due to improper policies enforced by the resident data-processing department. These restrictive policies were condoned by a weak or unknowing user management who did not realize what they could do or were not willing to fight the data-processing establishment for their right to use computer power.

Used properly, the "report-processing" concept is capable of providing a Free Enterprise computing-service environment. However, placed in the hands of a data-processing organization that is not enlightened enough to see the possible benefits to be derived from a Free Enterprise, user-oriented computer service, its effectiveness can be severely stifled. The report-processing system functional capability then is treated as a language and doled out to the user in the same way that programming has been. In other words, users specify their needs to planners, planners translate for the programmers, and programmers structure report-processing functions for problem solutions. The whole data-processing establishment is then a filter between the computer and the end-user. The powerful report-processing system tools of coordination and control make the prohibitive data-processing department very effective in establishing structured report-processing system use.

If, however, user management is wise enough to insist on and enforce the establishment of a Free Enterprise computer service, then major benefits can be obtained. The potential of computer power in full and effective use can be achieved throughout the operation.

The remainder of this chapter *examines* the uses of report processing (*reporting*) concepts. It will delineate good use and bad use; use that attains maximum results through encouragement of a user-oriented, Free Enterprise computing environment, and use that restricts and stifles such an environment.

The reasons behind the good and bad results are explained. The primary advocacy will be for the users. After all, they are the ones to be served by computers. Serving their needs is the only real justification for the data-processing industry and all data-processing departments. That may sound like such a basic truth that it should not have to be mentioned. But, unfortunately, there are many users in the world who will heartily agree that their data-processing deaprtment needs to be reminded. This book examines the characteristics of an enlightened data-processing service that successfully blends a Free Enterprise reporting service with conventional structured systems to provide total, computerized information processing.

In keeping with the concept of "free enterprise," final responsibility for data quality and synchronization is a user-community responsibility. Quality, timeliness, and accuracy of the data in reports are the responsibility of the report owners. In general, it is assumed that reports are kept up to date on a real-time basis. Events are reported immediately when they occur. To the extent that this is true, data retrieved by other cognizant users will be as up to date and accurate as is practical in real-time. Thus randomly sampled data should be suitable for most reporting purposes. Except for clerical errors that may be found in any data base or occasional delinquencies in timeliness for up to twenty-four hours (depending on the nature of the reporting process), a high level of data quality should be attainable in real-time. The convenience and facility to maintain a clean data base exists in a report-processing system.

Actual maintenance quality is subject to management discipline. Report-processing data in an unstructured application can be made inaccurate as easily as information in a manual document-processing system can be made erroneous. However, in general, data in a reporting-system data base will be more correctly reflective of the real world than structured, highly edited systems will be. The reason this is true is that the user depends on the base for real operational control. The users live in the base. It is the primary tool for maintaining control of the operation. Operations management stresses the need for accurate reflections and insists on timeliness and completeness. Events are reported as they are occurring without the lengthy time lag of batch-updated systems. This in itself represents a major improvement in accuracy. Without the up-to-date information representation, real-control is confused. With it, accuracy comes naturally. If errors are noted, they are immediately corrected rather than preparing a correction entry and seeing it in effect in the base tomorrow with the error present until correction takes place. Direct access to the report data for review, update, and correction are essential keys to timely data and accuracy. By directly scanning report data and especially the records adjacent to the desired one, continuous validation by use and observation of interrecord relationships are accomplished.

In a report-processing system, the form integrity and alpha-numeric edits upon data entry provide a great improvement in accuracy at the intial point of data entry. As data is transmitted in, automatic edit checks are made to ensure no form deviations, illegal header data, or field-boundary violations. The assurance is also provided that no alpha data gets into a quantity or dollar field or that certain data cannot be left out. If an attempt is made to enter data that violates these edit checks, the input is stopped and the cursor is immediately placed on the offending input character, and a diagnostic statement is presented on the screen indicating corrective action required. Such general edits are provided with no system structuring and without programming through the process of *form generation.*

Usually, form protection and simple combinations of alpha-numerical-character edit will suffice for most applications. However, if desired, an application can be as tightly edited as is required. These might include checks such as the validity of the name or number or date, or ascertaining whether the specification is within a legitimate range or of a specific kind.

In general, reporting-system coordinators cannot be responsible for the quality, accuracy, or timeliness of data in reports; this must remain the user's responsibility. However, they will intervene in cases of flagrant poor quality of data, especially if there is some pattern of repetitive defects that imply generally inadequate data-base management by the users.

System policies should not encourage the establishment of artificial cut-off dates on which reporting processes are to be finalized and temporarily frozen for sampling (retrieval) purposes. Preferred is a natural environment in which data is "as good as is practical" at all times. Events should be reported immediately as they occur. Setting up artificial cut-off dates will cause tendencies to save data for input near those dates rather than making efforts to be ready for sampling at any time. Thus, setting up dates can detract from real-time data quality. Also, abnormal input peak workloads requiring overtime and so on are often created by such artificial date boundaries. Factors of panic, stress, and confusion are unnecessarily introduced into the situation. Real-control information exists only where immediate reporting of current events is taking place. Accuracy and the real-time characteristics of data are best fostered in a natural, active environment where events are recorded as they occur and errors are corrected as they are detected.

Through Free Enterprise Computing concepts, a report-processing system can conveniently and easily provide reporting processes that are tailored to particular areas of functional operating responsibility. It can therefore be assumed that the best-quality data is attainable because it is prepared by those directly responsible for the relative functions. It is not only prepared by them, it is also used by them. Therefore, system coordinators will always recommend that extracts of data be made from bases closest to the functional responsibility. Information passed through layers of bureaucracy not directly involved with the source only generates misunderstanding unnecessarily.

5 An Unstructured, Real-Time, Reporting Application

The most common type of application for which a report-processing system is used is an application that can be called *unstructured*. This application is processed with general-purpose report-processing functions such as search, sort, match, and calculate. Such an application allows access to the original report data base for direct updating on the screen or by using match and search-update functions.

The only disciplines involved in such an unstructured application are those that ensure form integrity for the data as well as a character-type (alpha, numeric) edit on input. No validation of input data such as checking for legitimate dates or item numbers is done in such unstructured applications. Base cleanliness is ensured by the fact that users live in the base on a day-to-day, minute-to-minute basis. They use the base in real-control of their immediate operations. By utilitarian necessity, the base must reflect reality; therefore, it is kept correct through constant use and immediate correction and a persistent managerial insistence on accuracy.

A further characteristic of the unstructured reporting application is that the up-to-date report "data" is turned into information as transient demand occurs by the execution of the general-purpose report-processing functions such as search, sort, and compute. In other words, as questions of operational control develop, they are answered by the execution of the appropriate report-processing function or series of functions executed "on the fly." This is of course the only way that real, detailed, ground-floor control of operations can be obtained. This is a highly unstructured operational environment, and therefore, the only comptuer processing that can serve it is one that can be used in an unstructured manner. This is Free Enterprise computing of the highest order and utmost importance. It holds the greatest potential for broad-scale operational impact and productivity improvement.

Some of the unstructured reporting applications will have report-generating (RPG) functions developed for use with them. This is frequently done whre a repeating pattern of manually executed functional use occurs. Usually this is a pattern of data analysis. In such a case, the pattern of functional use is defined in the shorthand language of report-generator (RPG) function design as a procedural list in a report data set. The report is then registered with a prescribed name. The call of this name can then cause the list of functions to be executed in the prescribed manner. However, most of the reporting applications will not use RPGs but will be processed by the execution of manually executed functions.

Life Cycle of an Unstructured Report-Processing Application

To gain an appreciation of what constitutes an unstructured report-processing application, an examination of the typical life cycle of such an application would be instructive. It all begins as a gleam in the eye of someone in the operations area. Someone in the end-user environment becomes aware of report-processing techniques and recognizes that his or her manual information processing would be greatly improved by using a computerized report-processing system as an alternate method. Once such a service is generally in use in the area, such opportunities usually occur spontaneously and are primarily the result of word-of-mouth recommendation and pride-of-ownership demonstration within the user community. Typically, this is the best form of propogation of report-processing services. Need seeks invention, and a natural attraction to report processing usually generates the healthiest applications. A valuable stimulus to this environment is an abundant opportunity to see and learn about generalized report-processing capabilities with the tutorial aids of the system. However, the end determination of need and appropriate design is left in the user's domain.

A user-supportive, report-processing system-coordination function can be of great benefit in seeing that report-processing services are offered in the potentially most fertile areas of the operation. This is best done by a coordinator with real operating-environment experience. This proper exposure ensures the earliest productivity improvement in the most labor- and material-intensive areas, thus ensuring the earliest payoffs and most effective priorities of implementation.

Once the user has identified a potential concept of report processing, it is brought to the attention of the reporting-systems coordinator. The coordinator provides a sounding board for analyzing these embryonic concepts and is in a position to initially ensure that:

The idea warrants real-time report-processing services.

The information is not already existing in other bases.

There are substantial benefits (savings) to be had from real-time processing of this information.

The data-base organization plan is sound.

All user-community concerns are taken into account.

The system impacts are considered.

The user is aware of proper rules of design and system use.

If the proposed application seems generally well conceived, based on these initial evaluations, a user design and detailed plan definition is implemented. To accomplish this, a loosely edited, experimental, "free-form" report with blank field headers is made available for the user to design the layout or form of the reporting. A "form-design guide" aids the user in entering form, edit, and header definitions.

The user-designer should enter the required form and edit definitions along with examples of representative data into the experimental report using CRT display input. It is imperative that this design work be done on the display. It is not accepted if submitted on paper. Only by seeing and using the proposed information in its final supporting media can an effective design be made. Data rolled, shifted, updated, and positioned on a CRT display has a greatly different feel and perspective than it has written or printed on paper. It is also recommended that the data be printed and examined in the form of a computer printout. Again, the appearance of the data in printed form can influence the design perspective.

The user-designer should discuss the application design with all who will be involved in its use. These users will often indicate other considerations, needed data elements, and use requirements and dimensions that make the design more complete. A key factor in the design work is that it must be done by the user community that is directly involved. It should *not* be done for them. Only users have the intimate operational knowledge needed to convert this knowledge to an effective design. Nonuser planners will dilute design effectiveness.

Not only do attempts to communicate such knowledge to other system designers or programmers confuse the process, they make it much more time consuming and expensive. The design process can easily be understood and is best done by members of the user community. The requirement bugs, so prevalent in conventional systems, are greatly reduced with the user-design approach.

While the design process is in progress, a detailed plan for the proposed application is developed. This process is aided by the use of an "application definition and request" form. Elements of the application plan that must be defined are:

Title and description of the application.

A definition of the alternative method to report processing.

Estimates of alternate system costs (this provides a basis for assessing potential savings in the proposed application).

Estimates of historical-data requirements.

Estimates of update frequency and report-processing use (this aids in assessing system impacts).

Estimates of display-terminal and special dial-up requirements.

Definitions of any special security considerations.

Estimates of the size of the proposed data in terms of lines of data and quantity of reports.

In determining the size of the proposed base, a key consideration is the flow of data into and out of the base. New items will be entered into the base, and they will be tracked there during processing. As they become closed transactions, they must be removed from the base and treated as historical information. Thus the true size of the base is that represented in the average number of items on-line that represent new items, items in process, and recently closed items. It is basic to the plan and essential to the health of the application that a flow of information into and out of the base be maintained. The life of any viable control-information system requires a flow of new transactions in and a removal of inactive (historical) data or the application will be saturated with old data and become inoperable. This is especially true in the case of real-time information processing. Only a base clean of deadwood will remain responsive and effective. Active data should not have to be processed with historical data. Once information becomes historical data, it must be separated from the active information.

Historical data can be usually quickly removed by use of a search-update process, pulling the items on the basis of a closed-transaction code or perhaps on the basis of date reference and then, after copying them to a suitable record medium, deleting them. Usually printouts of such items are adequate. Other methods that can be used are cassette tape, magnetic tape, or diskette storage. If the historical data must be accessed frequently and the on-line storage space can be justified, the closed items can be searched out and moved to a type of reporting set up for historical reference purposes. The most common method is to allow the data to recede into the tape history that is automatically produced by the report-processing system on a daily basis.

The plan definition is made by the users initially and finalized in a coordination review. This will ensure that proper historical, base size, and flow considerations are included. It will ensure that the concept is soundly conceived and that system resource and safety considerations are observed.

When the form definition on the experimental report is completed and has been reviewed by all the potential users, it is submitted to the system coordinator for final approval and review. At this time checks to ensure that form standards defined in the form-design guide were observed in the form design. Standards such as date format, item definition, and coding systems standards are enforced. If all is in agreement, then production turn-on can proceed.

Form generation is the process that accomplishes what must typically be done by the programmer in the conventional structured application. The process is simple, requiring only minutes to accomplish. It involves submitting the headers from the layout in the experimental report made by the user application designer as input to the form-generation process. Edit choices and presentation formats are also entered. Once completed, the form of the reporting has been automatically locked in and will be protected during all input and report processing. The data-base definitions have been established, and all subsequent use will be backed up with recovery and history protection automatically.

This form-generation process accomplishes in minutes what takes conventional structured programmers many months to accomplish. What has been accomplished is the turn-on of a real-time reporting application that will have fast response time and will be updated in real-time and will be randomly and concurrently accessed and processed. Such application programming is of the most sophisticated sort. This is not a simple batch-processed COBOL application.

The implications of this ability to implement true, real-time, transaction-oriented applications are far reaching and important. An enormous new dimension of computer service is opened, for only with such quick, simple application turn-on can the myriad real-control applications in all operations be computerized. The savings over conventional real-time programming methodologies are potentially enormous. Also, ease of implementation means ease of application modification. This is essential to meet the ever-present forces of change engendered by new policies, needs, and expanded experience and visibilities provided by the new computer-processing capabilities. An evolutionary concept of real-time application development is supportable. The ability to implement applications quickly, learn from the implementation, and quickly enhance the application is possible.

Specifying in Free Enterprise Computing
Application Design

When the language used to create the computer application is so simple that the user can be the architect of his or her own systems, the requirements of translation are essentially nonexistent (see figures 18-1 and 18-2 in chapter 18). Therefore, the roles of system analyst, planner, and programmer are also unnecessary. If documentation is required at all, it is usually only required after design for procedural documenting purposes, the primary purpose of such documents being to provide data form and coding definitions and to ensure consistency and continuity in use during personnel transitions.

The simple specification requirements are attributable to the nature of Free Enterprise Computing. In the application-design phase, the concept of the end requirement exists in the mind of the user-designer and evolves during design and use. Organization of the information within the simply conceived, report-structured data base is a simple user process. The functional language of report processing is used in a design procedure that is essentially evolutionary. The user-architect does not have to predefine every question to be asked. As the questions occur, he or she selects from the repertoire of report-processing functions the tools needed to derive the answer to the question at hand. By executing these functions in real-time to accomplish the task, he or she is actually programming the computer on the fly or in what is described as an "interactive mode" of operation.

When the language of processing is so simple that the end-user can directly make the computer perform his or her tasks, should this even be called "computer programming"? Or is it simply "using the computer"? The computer is, after all, a machine. It is just a powerful tool. When users can influence it directly, making it perform tasks under their immediate direction, is this not simply using computers? When they can define the logic paths immediately and evaluate each step as it is accomplished, making decisions based on results produced and choosing new paths of logic, causing the computer to follow the paths seen, is this not simply using computers? Why give it a scientific, professional mystique and call it "programming"?

This question does have certain social significance. For instance, in operations where programmers are unionized, it is important to define what constitutes "programming" and what is simply "computer use". Where the language lines are drawn will have impact on existing or potential power structures. Must an end-user join a union simply because he or she is using a system in which every question to be posed, the logic of the solution, and form of presentation of the answer is not predefined and prestructured? Must he or she be in a union because he or she selects appropriate functions from a list and executes them to solve the informational requirements? If so, then users of hand calculators should also be considered "programmers."

The process of interactive problem solving is not a rigidly structured procedure. The minute-to-minute processing of real-control information is also not structured. It requires spontaneously devised logic derived on the basis of influences of the moment. Such procedures cannot be predefined. Preparation of specifications in advance of such problem solution is not only nonproductive but unnecessarily limiting. Once the functions of computer command are so simple and natural that they can be defined and executed by the end-user, the pseudoscientific aura that requires professional interpretation is gone. So goes the programmer, the systems analyst, the systems planner, and so goes the specification specialist relative to Free Enterprise computing applications.

6 Report-Processing System Coordination

Free Enterprise Computing, as found in the report-processing system concepts, requires a new kind of system-management skill. It is fulfilled at report-processing system sites by the role of a system coordinator. This is a type of system-management discipline that is a hybrid of skills from the user community as well as data processing. It is crucial that this coordinator function be properly administered in a way that fosters and supports a free-enterprise environment in a particular report-processing service.

A free-enterprise society operating without any governmental discipline is anarchy. A lawfully functioning goverment protects willing exchange and restrains unwilling exchange. Fraud, misrepresentation, and predatatory practices are penalized. Government's legitimate purpose is to codify and then inhibit all destructive actions while leaving all creative and productive actions to the performance of free citizens. This is an ideal level of governmental control. Obviously, however, even with a constitution such as ours, which is filled with clauses and amendments designed to restrict unhealthy governmental growth, excessive governmental bureaucracies are created and burdensome taxes and controls are established.

When the government takes over the operation of businesses, it negates the energy and stimulation and disciplines of free-enterprise, and the result is a loss of extra-individual efforts with the summed results suffering. Adam Smith, an economist of nearly two centuries ago, explained in his book *The Wealth of Nations* published in 1776:

> It is only for the sake of profit that any man employs a capital in the support of industry; and he will always, therefore, endeavor to employ it in the support of that industry of which the produce is likely to be of the greatest value. . . . He generally, indeed, neither intends it promote the public interest, nor knows how much he is promoting it. . . . By directing that industry in such a manner as its produce may be of greatest value, he intends only his own gain, and he is in this, as in many other cases, led by an invisible hand to promote an end which has no part of his intention. Nor is it always the worse for society that it has no part in it.

Adam Smith's invisible hand functions through *all* the individuals dealing in the free market. This is why it represents a working process that is capable of perpetually adjusting and improving mankind's economic situation for the good. Governments can never hope to achieve these perfections of control, but they can and do upset these functions by their interferences.

In a properly coordinated, Free Enterprise Computing environment, when the end-user designs his application, he functions in much the same manner as the entrepreneur in the free-market system. He directs computer power as much as he can to make his parochial operational environment more efficient. He does not intend to promote the common corporate data base but by efficiently managing and processing his immediate operational control information, he creates an accurate, clear, dependable subset of corporate data. This effective information processing enables him to productively manage his operation. Thus he is led by "an invisible hand" to provide operational information that is truly reflective of reality. Coincidentally, by automating his manually processed paper mills, he contributes to corporate productivity and profitability.

When computerized report processing is applied by the end-user in his environment, he fashions it to serve his most pressing current informational needs. Thus the greatest benefit is immediately obtained at the level that is most labor and material intensive. The application is usually successful because there are none of the usual communication problems in translating the need into computer performance through computer professionals. If oversights in design are made, the user designer is directly responsible and must accept responsibility. He cannot complain to others that they missinterpreted his requirements. For this to work, the language must allow convenient application correction and modification as report-processing systems do. In fact, most applications are not perfect in initial conception and must be enhanced and adjusted to obtain full potential. In any case, ultimately, the application must be modified to meet the requirements of operational change.

As users are initially developing their reporting applications, they have a natural tendency to restrict use and access to their immediate departments. Then as confidence in their information develops they provide access (usually read only) to other departments. Then, as the value of interdepartmental input and exchange becomes apparent, agreements to allow pertinent updating and access by outside users are made. Often interdepartment-application mergers are negotiated and consumated. Thus a sharing of operational-level bases naturally evolves. Also, as departmental bases accurately reflect reality, the department managers derive their status reporting to their superiors from that information. The manager or his people design report generations for this upward-status reporting. Thus efficiency and reporting accuracy is enhanced. A similar pattern of report-generating development percolates up through the management levels.

Ultimately, then, an operation-wide, computerized management-information system evolves that works. It works because it was developed from the bottom up by the users. True real-time computer power is implemented throughout the organization with the best possible set of priorities and benefit realization. Management (end-users) control the application design so it works and keeps working because they will adjust their uses to meet new operational policies, directions, or growth potentials. This approach prevents the situation that occurs commonly where extensive, conventionally structured systems calcify and even direct operation policy instead of remaining passively utilitarian.

In the free-market system, too much governmental interference and control stifles incentives and can be seriously detrimental to the innovative nature and effectiveness of enterprise. So, too, a coordination function that overcontrols the users can seriously reduce the inventive catalytics and implementation effectiveness in a report-processing system environment. The ideal atmosphere to be created is one in which an *illusion* of infinite capability is developed for the end-user to operate within. Freedom of processing choice is allowed within the planned size and scope of his or her reporting application. This scope is planned in conjunction with system coordination, the related impacts are justified with expected payoffs, then actual use is monitored to ensure performance according to plan.

Ideally performed, a reporting-system coordination function should: *Establish and support a productive report-processing service that allows the greatest possible degree of user freedom in processing choice while ensuring system safety and security and an effective use of system resources.* Not all existing report-processing services are ideally coordinated. In fact, the ideal is more the exception than the rule. In the early days of reporting-system development, the coordinator functioned in a primarily intuitive manner. He or she relied on manual sampling techniques, rumor, and vague descriptions of how users thought they were using the system. Analysis with the general report-processing functions and a lot of basic detective work were the tools of trade. Today's coordinator can be omniscient and omnipotent in the management of the report-processing service he or she administers.

An extensive array of security techniques are available to provide almost any needed protection against improper data access or system abuse. Users as well as terminals are registered and controlled individually. Users may be restricted to any level of functional capability if desired. All transactional activity is logged. Real-time and batch analyzers are available for transactional monitoring. Real-time and batch analyzers of communications errors and use are also provided by communications-system management. Many real-time and batch processes are available to aid the reporting-system coordinator in system control and data-base management. The functional report-processing capabilities are used extensively to provide effective real-time control of the report-processing service.

Indeed, the visibilities and controls available to the system coordinator are all encompassing. Not only is total control possible but a tendency to overcontrol is also prevalent. This is especially noticeable at sites where the service is dominated by a strong data-processing establishment that has traditionally been a sole source provider of computer services to a tightly disciplined user-community. At such sites the full potentials of Free Enterprise Computing are not attained. Due to the unncessarily restrictive policies invoked, innovation and flexibility is stifled. The resultant losses to productivity, operational efficiency, and adaptability are high, unfortunate, avoidable, and costly.

The improperly restrictive coordination function is usually created when the report-processing service is delivered through a highly developed data-processing organization. Such an organization with its cadres of data-processing group managers, managers, supervisors, consultants, planners, system analysts, programmers, and documentation specialists see a Free Enterprise, user-oriented, real-time, reporting service as a distinct threat to the data-processing establishment. They have been indoctrinated to an idea that only structured use designed by data-processing professionals is effective computer use. The idea of a system that allows the turn-on of real-time reporting applications in minutes instead of months is clearly threatening. True real-time updating of original report data is not easy to design into any structured system, and here it is offered automatically with each new application. The idea of not having to predefine all questions to be asked so that the solution path can be structured by program disciplines for utmost efficiency is unthinkable. Turn the users loose in a so called real-time Free Enterprise, random-access report-processing system with real-time updating of original report data supported? This is clearly revolutionary and threatening to the data-processing professional group.

Can using computers be this easy? Programming is obviously not easy. It is a professional skill requiring extensive training of a mind talented to observe logical intricacies. How could this science be reduced to a simple language that end-users can manage? Unthinkable? The data-processing professional who has attended all those programming and system-design schools, who has attended endless seminars on programming and system-design efficiencies, and who has experienced the complex logic of major system design has the greatest difficulty in understanding a Free Enterprise approach to report processing. Just as the entrenched governmental bureaucrat cannot envision how a free-market system can function without their intervention and control, so the data-processing professionals often have trouble understanding a real-time, user-oriented approach to information processing. Acting in fear and this lack of understanding, data-processing establishes and insinuates unnecessary restrictions and controls in providing the service. Due to these smothering influences, the operation loses the potential for ingenuity, innovation, and adaptation.

The way to ensure an improper reporting coordination function is to assign a person with only a data-processing or programming background and have the coordination position report directly to data-processing management. The less familiar the coordinator is with the real needs of the user operations (not the needs as perceived by data processing), the less chance there is that a successful control will be established. An ideal candidate for reporting coordination would be a person with extensive operational experience in the user-community along with some data-processing skills. Such skills are an asset in dealing with system support and data-processing personnel. These skills are also valuable in consideration of report-processing use in relation to structured systems as well as in developing interfaces for data passage between reporting systems and other systems in the computing environment.

The primary business of report-processing coordination is user control. Therefore, real knowledge of the requirements of the operation is the prime requirement. With this experience, a coordinator can effectively direct the report-processing services with the best set of priorities into the areas where greatest benefits can be achieved most rapidly. He will be most sensitive to user concerns, and he will be able to talk their language. Coordination and communication with the end-user community go hand in hand.

Ideally, the coordinator should report directly to operations management. The most successful, established report-processing services are those where this reporting relationship exists. At least, the coordination function must be strongly supported by management in developing a Free Enterprise Computing environment.

Effective coordination means a minimum of obstructive meddling in user processing. Only when such processing significantly exceeds planned application scope should coordination become an obstructive influence. The key to the entire concept of effective report-processing system coordination is embodied in the concept that the resource impact and scope of use of each application is planned in terms of use and data-base characteristics. Then as the application is developed and put into productive use, it is monitored to assure performance to plan. Thus plan/actual use analysis and data-base control is accomplished. A coordinator exercizes two different vectors of influence on the user-community. First, he or she functions as a stimulator to accelerate application implementation. Then when the applications are fully operating, he or she acts as a governor to the user-innovator, identifying deviations from planned use and bringing influences to bear which then return an aberrant application back to plan. To gain further insight into the function of report-processing system coordination, the following general overview of the job of coordinator is presented.

Reporting-System Coordinator: General Job Description

The job of report-processing system coordinator involves the general control of use of the reporting service as it relates to the design, implementation, use, and development of the reporting data base and interface of these reports to other application files in the system. It involves coordination with the present and potential system users within the central-system location and on remote terminals accessing the reporting data base. The coordinator is responsible for planning, preparing, and implementing demonstration and training exercises for present and potential users. He or she must coordinate data-base use and development with other support personnel to eliminate conflicts with the central-system hardware and software modification and other application change. He or she is responsible for establishing and administering data-base security techniques. In his or her role, he establishes a central point for system-use information and coordination.

Related Tasks

1. The system coordinator must compare planned and actual usage of the report data bases to total system capability to ensure efficient, effective utilization. This comparison is made by checking the known system-storage and communication-system capacities against daily reports defining actual system utilization. These studies allow the coordinator to ensure effective reporting applications and to predict and plan for system enhancements and expansion requirements. He or she ensures that proper security controls are used relative to the data base.
2. The coordinator determines the needs and desires of local and remote users of the report data base and priorities for proposed report processing applications. He or she must obtain a definition of the justification for new reporting applications. He or she performs application turn-on and formating procedures to implement new reporting processes. He or she monitors the application in process and takes necessary administrative action to ensure effective use according to plan.
3. The coordinator must plan and provide demonstrations and training exercises for present and potential system users. He or she administers user registration and security controls related to users.
4. The coordinator defines hardware requirements based on user feedbacks, anticipated-use levels and present system capacities as well as new hardware capabilities. He or she assists the system-support group in obtaining authorization and funding approval for such hardware.
5. He or she must plan, execute, and monitor systems growth to assure hardware availability in a timely manner without undue disruption of present-system service during installation.

6. The coordinator is responsible for the general scheduling of the system service. This includes defining for the users system operating time and availability as well as the timing of data linkages to other systems.

7. The coordinator is responsible for procuring and disseminating the system and terminal-operating guidelines to the users. The coordinator must be aware of all types of reporting done in the base and be cognizant of other application data bases that are in the computing system. He or she will assist and encourage the users to avoid or eliminate the duplication of data by using a proper interface of these data bases.

7

The Evolution of a User: Report-Generator (RPG) Designer

A remarkable phenomenon among the users who have developed their functional expertise sufficiently to become RPG designers is their strong insistence that they do not consider RPG design to be programming. They are very clearly opposed to the idea that when they design RPGs, they are acting as programmers. The reaction is remarkably consistent among users. It is evident among those who are not familiar with data processing at all as well as among those users who have had training in data processing and even some with programming experience in COBOL, Fortran, or BASIC languages.

They see their primary contribution to the solution of a problem as their operational expertise and their intimate knowledge of the input parameters of the problem to be solved. To them, the language of reporting seems to be "the way computers are supposed to be used." Once the language seems natural to use, the professional mystique of programming evaporates. All that remains is getting the job done and using the computer as just another tool for analyzing, computing, and information gathering.

It is worth noting that all report-processing system users will not become RPG designers. It is a technique that appeals to the user who is motivated to obtain full benefit from report-processing capabilities. Often a fascination develops to learn and use report-processing techniques to the fullest. If this motivated user is also gifted with a degree of innovative talent and a somewhat logical mind, the person then possesses the potential for becoming a capable RPG designer. Such motivation and talent does not appear in all users, but it is sufficiently abundant in the end-user community. Some users are smart enough to be motivated and challenged by fascinating logic. Some can also be ingeniously innovative. These characteristics are not restricted to the mind with a computer-science degree. One of the most exciting aspects of watching proper, user-oriented, Free Enterprise Computing implementation in a user-community is to see the multifaceted ingenuity and innovative adaption of computing power in the report-processing environment. This is especially noteworthy among the users who develop into RPG designers.

At first appearance, a control statement made in the RPG function language would appear to be somewhat heiroglyphic, even programmer-like. However, it must be remembered that the user will be intoduced to RPG design language training only after he or she has evolved to what can be called a "sophisticated user" of manually executed report-processing functions.

Such a user will have been through the basic training process. With a display, he or she will have interactively processed a demonstration data base that was designed to illustrate most of the more popular general report-processing capabilities. He or she will have used all the manually executable report-processing functions available to general users. Besides learning what these functions can do, he or she will have been given an appreciation of the nature of the report-oriented data base. He or she will also have been exposed to the options usable with the various functions and will have an appreciation of what information-processing powers can be derived from their use.

With this general functional training accomplished, the user becomes a production user, processing live data in a real production environment. Here he or she learns the realities of functional report processing. By actually adapting report-processing functions to the solution of real-world production problems, he or she gains an intimate knowledge of capabilities of the functions he or she chooses and executes. By trial and sometimes by error, he or she learns what report-processing functions and their options will do in production problem solving. Since these functions are the "instructions" of the report-generation language, the user possesses an invaluable insight that ideally serves him or her in accomplishing effective RPG design.

The user is aided and reinforced in this learning process by the availability of self-grading, on-line examinations that are designed to identify any weaknesses he or she may have in his or her basic report-processing training. He or she also has access to documented display-operating procedures that can be selectively referred to on-line as required. With the self-teaching tutorial aids, reinforcing exams and procedural references, a self-fulfilling learning environment is created in which each user can rise to a proficiency level according to his or her need, talent, and relative motivation. From this catalytic world of production users, those with RPG designer potential identify themselves.

If one looks at the language of report-generator design from the normal perspective of a "sophisticated user" who knows his or her accessible data bases, the nature of the general report-processing functions, their characteristics, strengths, and options, and the realities of general-purpose, real-time, report-processing production, then the transition to an understanding of the report-generator design language is not a mysterious step to heiroglyphic symantics. Instead, it seems to be a natural next step to more functional power and to a shorthand way of using the same functions that are already so familiar. The RPG language is designed to support this transitional attitude.

The flow of the manually executed function is the same as the pattern of definition for the report-generator control statement. Because of this similarity of pattern, it is easy to see how the user can easily learn this language, for it is indeed merely a shorthand way of prescribing the report-processing functions they are so familiar with.

So it becomes more and more difficult to say what constitutes functional uses of computers and where true programming begins. One can understand how it is difficult and even incorrect for a user-report-generator designer to claim to be a programmer. It is possible to understand the users' insistence that they are not programmers when using the report-generation design language. They do not consider themselves to be programmers when they manually cause the functions to be executed. So why should simply setting the same function up in a different way for execution cause them to suddenly be classified as programmer? Probably the most important reason to not call them programmers is that their real career is that associated with their work in the operation. They are simply users of computer power with new skills used in conjunction with their main profession.

8 Coordination of Report-Generator Design and Use

A report-processing system coordination that is too heavily influenced by a restrictive data-processing organization tends to reduce the potential effectiveness of a report-processing service in a number of ways. Report-generator design and use is an area in which a restrictive data-processing management usually establishes the tightest restrictions and thereby does the greatest damage to the potential benefits of a Free Enterprise, report-processing service. Much of data-processing management has great difficulty with the idea of letting users be report-generation designers. Their initial reaction is that report-generator design should be restricted to professional programmers. Of course, this does not mean that only programmers get into the act. The whole DP-approval cycle, analysis bureaucracy, planners, system analysts, and documenting specialists are also brought into the design process.

Often there is a great deal of empire protection behind this restrictive attitude toward report-generator design. But frequently too there is simply a failure to understand that the report-generator language is merely a form of shorthand for controlling the use of the report-processing system's manually executable functions. The majority of user report-generator designers do write report-generator applications that are essentially functional sequences. Granted, there is much more than functional sequencing capability in report-generator design, but most users accomplish most of their design with functional sequences. These are easily controlled and managed to assure effective use. The more talented, ingenious user report-generator designers will use the full potential of the more intricate report-generator design techniques. But there again it is their innate talent that makes this design work that is well done. It is these user-designers who produce the most productive, exciting applications of report-generation use. Due to the coordination controls available for the report-generation design process, the design process is system safe and productive whether the users are superstar innovative talents or simply knowledgeable report-processing system users.

A strange phenomenon in the real world of report-generator design is the fact that professional programmers usually make poor report-generator designers. At first, this seems remarkable when one considers the proven, trained, professional data-processing mind. It is difficult to define precisely why programmers generally do poor report-generator design work. Probably, the lack of report-processing user orientation and experience in the programmer is the key factor. The typical user-turned-report-generator-designer is a highly experienced user of the manually executable report-processing functions. He or she knows what these functions do, their options, and real potentials. What is of utmost importance is the fact that he or she knows what they can do from actual use on his or her own report data. This implies not only operational experience with the report-generation instruction repertoire (the report-processing functions themselves) but also intimate data-base report-processing experience. He or she knows how the functions perform in use with his or her own live data base. He or she also enjoys the great advantage of knowing what the problem is that needs to be solved. He or she will solve only that problem neither doing more or less than is necessary.

Since the programmer usually is not a general-purpose, production user of the report-processing system, he or she neither has the operational knowledge of functional use nor is he or she intimately data-base knowledgeable. The professional programmer's data-processing expertise is often more of a disadvantage than an advantage. In learning new concepts, people naturally try to relate newly encountered ideas to what they have previously experienced. In the case of the data-processing professional, he or she often tries to handle the report data base as he or she has always handled the file-record structured bases, namely, one record at a time. The report-processing system's functions are designed to handle a set of records (an entire report) at one time. Report processing as a concept is often a problem for the data-processing professional to grasp due to his or her file- and record-processing experience.

If the programmer's background is in COBOL batch processing, he or she typically tries to use the real-time, transaction-oriented report-processing capabilities as a batch-processing language. Having little or no experience with transactionally processing information in real-time, he or she designs report generators that process hundreds of thousands or even millions of records as one transaction. Such batch-oriented design is actually dangerously detrimental to the performance of the real-time report-processing service.

The data-processing professional is used to processing files, not reports. Files tend to be big. Reports tend to be small, usually less than 500 lines in length. So a frequent error the data-processing report-generator designer makes is to put all the data into one report. This then is usually too large for suitable report processing. In real-time report processing, only one updater is allowed in a report at one time. So by putting all the data in one report, simultaneous updating accessibility by many users is prohibited. In the report data base, each report is an entry point for access. By breaking the base naturally into many small reports, the user not only creates the ability to support multiple, simultaneous updates, he or she has a base that is accessible at many points (the many reports individually). The data-processing designer, by lumping the data all into one report, limits updating, accessibility, and processing.

The data-processing designer is also by experience, a record, not a report, processor. To him or her, reports are the output from program executions, usually print listings, so when he or she faces a concept that processes reports, it is difficult to grasp. The user, however, clearly sees that his or her report is the final product of information and he or she clearly processes it, updates it, searches it, sorts it, and so on. The DP professional does his or her best to gain an understanding of report processing by using the tutorial cookbooks and demonstration data bases, but this is no substitute for the real-world user experience of production, real-time processing in the user-designed data base.

So the data-processing designer goes through the relatively sterile demonstration data-base learning process and assimilates enough of the basics to qualify for report-generator design school. He or she learns by rote the shorthand language for writing report-generator control statements. He or she is not really comfortable with search, sort, or compute statements because he or she was not comfortable with the use of these functions in the demonstration, tutorial base environment. Nevertheless, he or she goes down through the report-generator instruction (or function) list until encountering the read line, write line and IF logic capabilities. This he or she recognizes. His or her wealth of data-processing experience now comes to bear. He or she is home again and has found "read a record" (read line), "write a record" (write line), and with the logical IF, he or she proceeds to design report generators that are horribly inefficient. He or she constructs the instruction repertoire of report processing, the search, match, and compute functions using read line, write line, and IF logic and ignores as much as possible the less familiar but efficient and powerful functions already available and assembled in machine code.

On the other hand, the non-data-processing-oriented report-processing-system-user turned report-generator designer reverts to his or her base of experience and favors report-processing functions in design choices. The choices are good because he or she intimately knows their power in execution of his or her own data. The use of read lines and write lines occurs only when he or she cannot do the job with standard report-processing functions. Since the report-processing system is internally ideally geared to the execution of report-processing functions, these runs are simple in design and efficient in use.

In either case, be the report-generator (RPG) designer a programming professional, a talented user, or simply a user who has done his or her homework and is now doing RPG design, the tools are available for complete, system-safe control of the design process and production use of the report generators.

The process of control begins with user qualification to be an RPG designer. RPG design is a unique functional capability that can be turned on or off for a given user. So, once a candidate for RPG design has learned the characteristics of basic report-processing functions, their options and all the related powers they possess, they must prove this expertise by passing on-line proficiency exams with very high grades. Given this basic proof of general, functional knowledge, the potential RPG designer then usually attends a RPG design class that includes workshop solutions of example problems. With this schooling completed, the functional capability of RPG design is registered by the system coordinator for this user. The shorthand statements that define and control the functions to be executed in a given report generation are called *control statements*. They are entered as report data in a report data set. The report, which then describes the control statements or procedure to be executed, is registered and given a name that can be called to execute the report generation.

When the RPG control report is registered, a number of control characteristics are defined.

An RPG name is registered. This is the name that is entered to cause the RPG to execute.

The RPG can be set to run at only a given display station or selected stations.

The RPG can also be set to run by only a signed-on individual or individuals.

The RPG limitations relative to data-base security are set.

A fixed storage-access limit is set. This is an allowed quantity of read and write accesses (I/Os) to storage.

A logic line limit is set. This is allowed quantity of control-statement lines that will be read from the RPG control report and executed.

A flag is then set with the registration indicating that the RPG is in a design phase of development.

The whole process or RPG registration is done in real-time. It is usually done in minutes over the phone by the user requesting the registration to be done by the report-processing system coordinator.

Registration is then complete, and the user can begin design. If he or she is new to design work, he or she may elect to use some of the tutorial RPG design aids, which were discussed in class, that provide guidance in filling out the various parts of the RPG function control statements. He or she is also taught in RPG design class to set up a small sample test data base containing examples of all data elements. This will allow the full development of the logic of the RPG. This not only protects the original report data but creates a faster response time during the interactive debugging process.

As he or she completes the definitions of the control statements, they can be executed immediately to see if they perform correctly. If there are errors in defining the statements, the RPG fails, and the failing RPG control report is displayed starting at the failing instruction. A diagnostic statement appears at the top of the display indicating the nature of the error, and the cursor is placed on the offending field or subfield of the erring control statement. This design work is quickly done, and testing is equally fast because there is no waiting for assemblies, compiles, or diagnostic listings to be provided. As a general rule, as an indication of efficiency of this application design method, it can be said that a real-time, transaction-oriented application with real-time updating can be done in less time than it would take to prepare a program-design specification using conventional, structured programming methods. RPG design is typically one-fifth or less the time of conventional language design for a comparable real-time application.

It should be noted that he or she must complete this design testing in the allowed I/O and logic line limit set for this RPG at the time of registration. Working with the limited test data base, this can be done easily within the set limits. If he or she should exceed the I/Os or logic line limits, the RPG stops and gives a diagnostic message indicating that the I/O or logic line limit has been reached. An important point here is that this design environment is perfectly controllable and system safe. The I/O limits effectively control the allowance of system resource, and the logic line limit protects against computer consumption or endless loops. Data-base accessibility is also safely limited.

Eventually, the user finishes the design and testing of the RPG. He or she had been instructed when asking to have the RPG registered by the coordinator that the RPG was considered in design and that he or she would be expected to have the RPG "log analyzed" when design was done and ready to put into production. So when ready for analysis, he or she makes an entry in the RPG that turns on the detailed transaction-logging process for the RPG. He or she then executes the RPG, noting the start and stop time of the RPG. With this information, he or she contacts the coordinator, usually by phone, giving the station number at which the RPG was executed and the times of the RPG. The coordinator then uses the real-time log-analysis function on hand to extract those RPG-related transactions from the total transaction log. He or she now has a step-by-step, instruction-by-instruction, detailed picture of the RPG in execution. There are also RPGs designed to test RPG design quality, which the user can use to determine RPG design quality before requesting final anlaysis from the coordinator.

From this log data, the coordinator can evaluate the specific impacts of each instruction executed in terms of I/Os expended, lines of data processed, response time, and identity of report data processed. He or she has RPGs, which have been developed for coordinator use, that perform calculations on the log data. These calculations determine cost of the RPG in terms of resource dollars, and totals are developed for I/Os used, data and logic lines processed, response time, and other factors. From these analytical statistics, a very clear picture is established of the nature of the RPG, its effectiveness and system-resource impacts. At this point, if design improvements are suggested, the designer will be given the log analysis with suggestions on corrections to be made. The design-analysis interchange continues till the coordinator is satisfied that a sound RPG has been created. Realistic I/O and logic line limits are then set for actual production use.

Often these production limits can be lower than those allowed in the design phase. In a real world of random-access, real-time report processing, control is obtained by executing many small processes. This characteristic also holds true in RPG function use. The vast majority of RPGs are relatively small analytical porocesses. This is another fact that many batch-processing oriented, data-processing professionals have a hard time grasping. True real-time transactions-processing system experience is not that common among data-processing professionals. Most are familiar with larger batch-job control systems; they fail to appreciate the nature of the Free Enterprise Computing environment, which is really a seething sea of small transaction processing that can be seriously polluted with a batch-job-oriented control philosophy.

Some RPG functions can be developed that will do large amounts of data processing. They are designed in the same manner as other RPGs. After all the logic is developed, tested, and analyzed with a small test base, the RPG is allowed to execute against its full base with large-scale processing. To make this system safe, the I/O and logic line limits are established at appropriate larger settings. However, an allowed time of execution limit is established in addition to the other limits. This will allow the RPG to be executed only at nonbusy system times such as in the evening or over the noon hour. Such RPGs can also be scheduled to automatically start at a specific time perhaps well into second- or third-shift operation. A log analysis is also performed on the first execution under full-scale limits. With the knowledge from this analysis, the limits of I/O, logic lines, and time are ideally set for production use.

The development of RPG functions that process large amounts of data and provide extensive analytical power can often serve as a valuable initial design phase for the development of structured systems. For instance, a sizable RPG function may be developed that is providing an extensive data analysis and a resultant report generation in print-listed form. The simplicity of the RPG function language will enable the user to develop all the logic of the RPG and actually produce the desired result. Now it can be decided that this analysis could as easily be performed with a COBOL batch-report generator. Taking this type of large-scale report generation out of real-time system priority and running it at batch priority is obviously a better use of resources. Lower priority and larger data buffers make this batch-processing resource effective for massive data processing.

With the developed RPG for guidance, the process of designing the COBOL report generator is made much simpler. All the logic is specifically defined in the RPG as well as the data-base relationships. There is also no question that the form of the output is what is really wanted. Clearly, the whole process of structured program design is made much more efficient and the success of the effort more assured.

Analysis tools are also available to coordination to aid in monitoring production use of the RPGs. The entire transaction log record for each day is reduced to a record for each RPG indicating its frequency of use and highest I/O impact. These daily records are summarized on a weekly basis and on a monthly basis to establish a history of actual RPG use that provides a sound basis for RPG management. From these records, it is also possible to identify RPG functions that have become inactive and can be removed from the system.

So there is really no danger in allowing the users to become designers of report generators. A completely system-safe, controlled, fully limited design environment can be created. Visibility is provided to ensure efficient design, and use of the report generators can be monitored to ensure performance to plan and even to identify report generators that become inactive.

Clearly, there is no danger in involving the innovative members of the user-community in report-generator design. The real danger lies in not doing so. For then, that rich, innovative potential that exists in every user-community is stifled, and a burdensome, expensive data-processing bureaucracy is unnecessarily encouraged.

9

Data-Base Concepts and Standardization

When sciences become the province of professionals, there is a tendency to obscure the basic craft in semantics. Terms are invented to describe methods, and concepts. Also in complex professional sciences, precise systems are conceived to organize the methodologies. Individuals who then master these terms and systems conduct seminars at which the primary activity is defining these terms and systems for others.

These teachers and students then become the professionals as the sciences mature. Then, in an attempt to secure their professional establishment, these professionals congregate in committees to define which terms and systems are to be the standards for the relative science. Corporate political power is then enlisted to give force to the standardization. The thrust of this forced professional standardization then is to protect the establishment, and the effect is to stifle innovation and change and to force conformity.

That is a pretty harsh indictment of all standards concepts, and perhaps it is not totally justified, but there is a certain amount of truth there. Only when one considers the volatile nature of computer technology and the staggering advances in capability that have been achieved can one begin to understand why establishment of computing standards has been so controversial in this industry.

Thousands of manyears have been invested in standards committee meetings over the years in the evolution of the computer industry. Attempts have been made to standardize just about everything. In actuality, a great deal remains unstandardized even after all that effort.

Consider one of the areas of standardization that has firmed up in the computer industry and what some of the effects of this are. Specifically, consider data-base standards. These standards are becoming universally accepted among the data-processing professionals. The CODASYL committees, backed by corporate power, are establishing a general conformance. The remaining dissenters are relatively few.

However, let us carefully consider these generally accepted standards. Let us examine the evolution of data-base theory and data-base standards. To do this, we have to go back before the use of CRT-display terminals. We have to go back to a time when computers were primarily punch-card driven (would you believe that some computers are still primarily punch-card driven?). The main means of input then was by punched cards whether the holes were round or rectangular. Let us examine the first significant data-base concept of real consequence. This concept embodied the idea that a record made up of key fields of data and related subfields constituted a basic data set and that these records could be connected together with storage-address pointers to form what is referred to as a *data file*. This concept endured for a long time. Today we still talk about "processing files and records." But going back, remember, the concept was invented as being ideal data-base organization in a punched-card-driven computer environment.

The reason this concept was ideal for a system that was punch-card up-dated was because all updating was done in a batch mode of operation. Real-time random access was not done at all at that time. Batch processing of records was and still is a very efficient method. This is true because when files are loaded in storage, the files are usually ordered in some way—by part number, job number, customer number, name, address, and so on. So the data resides in storage in a neat, ordered way. This is called a *sequential file*.

Now when record updating had to be done, it was very easy and also very efficient. The record change data was collected and punched into cards. The cards were sorted into the same order as the records were organized in storage. Then when a mass or batch-record updating took place, a very efficient, single pass was made over the records with the changes being written in as the records were passed. It was very efficient and neat because of the similarly organized cards and record-storage order. It worked well because it was batch updating.

As long as the primary outputs were batch-processed print listings of record data, these techniques continued to be pretty efficient. But then the need for multipath record processing began to enter the picture. In other words, the record order of the file was not the only order of access that was required. So file indexing was introduced, and things became a little more complicated. Frequently multiple index levels were set up to provide multiple paths to the records. Basically, these were tables organized by data keys such as item numbers, status codes, and dates, and pointers were attached to these keys to point to the record or records in storage that related to each of these keys. The indexing gave a secondary advantage in that a single reference to a key data element such as a name could be stored in a table and pointers to all records related to that would avoid the necessity of repeating the name in all the related records. This had significant value in the earlier days when storage costs were very high.

This indexing technique did create the burden of index maintenance in addition to record updating. However, because these indexes were ordered and with correspondingly ordered batch updating, the process was still quite efficient.

Great impetus was given to index integration into the bases when real-time access became a major aspect of data-processing services. Speed of access was essential, and indexing was the obvious method to attain this. This record-indexed-file concept is capable of providing fast access. The characteristic to be looked up is located in a table that yields the pointer or pointers to the related record or records to be accessed. The record or records can then be accessed (read) directly with these pointers. The record-indexed-file structure provides fast access, but it comes apart under the need for extensive real-time updating. As records are randomly added or deleted from the file, linkages between records have to be adjusted. Also, the related index tables have to be expanded and contracted, and the keyed pointers must be changed. This becomes extremely demanding on system resources, especially where extensively cross-referenced pointers are involved. Record placement becomes scattered in storage as they are moved around, and the neat order and efficiency of file initiaiton dissolves under the demands of real-time, random-access record updating.

This then is the primary reason that today most large indexed data bases are batch updated and accessed for retrieval purposes only. As long as only batch updating is used, record and index order is retained and updating can be done efficiently. The indexed pointers make real-time retrieval access fast even to one of millions of records, but the more complex the indexing, the more predominant are batch update and real-time only retrieval characteristics. This is an industry wide phenomenon, and yet the basic concept of the unit-record-file conceived in a punch-card-driven computer era goes essentially unquestioned. This is true even though the predominant trends in today's information processing is to real-time updating and random access and a great need of flexibility to meet the forces of change.

Obviously, with multilevels of indexes, records, and access paths, organization of the record-pointer arrays becomes more and more complex, and efficiency in organization becomes more critical. Of course, anything as complex and susceptible to varying interpretation as these disciplines would be certain to attract those whose forte is to pontificate on symantics, systems, and standards. All this complexity and variance clearly represented the potential for the creation of significant new professions.

So we saw the evolution of the data-base profession. This really gained strength in the early seventies when the concept of Management Information Systems (MIS) and the so-called Common Corporate Data Base became the talk of the industry. The theories expounded identified information about a corporation's operations as being "corporate assets." This implied a tangibility and value that could be accounted for and controlled as if it were cash flow, capital goods, or real estate. Unfortunately, communication and the flow of real-control information in a dynamic corporation is about as predictable as weather and just as hard to change by outsiders to the operation.

But, myopically, the promotion of data-base concepts proceeded. These data-base "professionals" had the short-sightedness to suggest that there is a hierarchical relationship of data within a corporation that could be identified and simplistically diagrammed as a layered pyramid, the top layer being executive information, the middle layer being management information, and the bottom layer being operational information. They also ignored the realities of complexity and volatility inherent in corporate life when they pronounced that a data base could be designed in such a way that a relationship could be established and diagrammed linking all elements or records of data from the top of the pyramid to the bottom. This was dubbed the "Common Corporate Data Base." Theoretically, it was said to be uniquely efficient because it had "no redundancy of data"! For instance, all the data elements of a business transaction could theoretically be stored in such a way that pointers could related all elements to each other.

Naturally, in actual attempts to implement these data-base concepts, the complexities of information exchange caused the diagrams of elemental interrelationships to become so complex in implementation as to become true works of abstract art. Just to collect and identify these relationships of data flow represented countless manhours of committee research.

Selling this new science was no easy task, and dissertations on how to affect the implementation of a "Common Corporate Data Base" always started with exhortations on the need for placement of the management-information systems director at the highest corporate-management level; usually a vice president position was deemed ideal. This was considered essential because to collect and define all these patterns of elemental data relationships would require access to the most sensitive data and operational relationships in every department. Obviously, there would be strong resistance from some departments to such encroachments; hence the need for overwhelming corporate power. Sometimes information relationships were encountered in the real world that did not conveniently conform to these pristine, nonredundant data concepts. Abundant political power was then needed to force realistic information needs to fit the new, standardized molds as decreed by the high priests of MIS.

Some sizeable corporations actually accepted the concepts embodied in the Management Information System, Common Corporate Data Base, and spent millions of dollars to establish these within their corporations. Reports on the progress or lack thereof were regularly published, and those in the new profession of data-base managers watched with great anticipation.

Then, when some of these larger system attempts at creation of Common Corporate Data Base became well enough defined to attempt going into actual production, the harsh light of reality dawned. The inefficiencies and inflexibilities inherent in these concepts became starkly apparent.

Multimillion-dollar-system fiascos were reported. Great disenchantment developed in the user-community, and in a few cases where graceful dismantling of the systems was not practical, multimillion-dollar systems were actually thrown out.

A vast silence then descended upon the data-processing industry regarding these embarrassing concepts. There was a rush noted among the numerous MIS departments that had been established to become quickly disassociated with concepts of MIS and the Common Corporate Data Base. They changed their names from the "MIS Department" to others such as the "Data Processing Department," the "Information Services Department," or "Information Systems Department." Since most had not made much real progress in the new MIS disciplines, it was not too difficult to redirect their efforts and thereby give themselves the appearance of sensitive management.

But, having once attended all those MIS seminars and studies and having read all those books, the DP brains were considerably washed. They still attended their association meetings and still were faced with the infrastructures of pointers, tables, and record arrays resident in their file-record structured systems and data bases. So the drive and pressures were still there to systematize and professionalize data-base concepts.

This all resurfaced a few years later as the concept of the "Data Base Management System." One of the highest-paying jobs in data processing today is the "data-base manager of the Data Base Management System." Of course, these "new" concepts are the talk of the industry again. The standards committees have blessed them, and we are heading toward the, supposedly, inevitable world of the "Integrated Data Base." Would you believe that this is a base in which redundancy is eliminated and all data or record relationships are established via pointer arrays now called "schemas"? We change, and yet we do not change!

High-level corporate backing is needed to support the implementation of these concepts. Redundancy of data is not allowed. All data relationships in a corporation can supposedly be diagrammed and programmed or "integrated" into computer-storage "schemas." However, if one listens carefully, complaints regarding the same problems of efficiency and inflexibility can be frequently heard. Methods of improving efficiency are being devised and promoted. One of these is a concept of "data dictionaries," a new system for organizing the pointer arrays that define the interelement data relationships. Also, some day, something called the "Data Base Computer" will greatly speed up pointer processing.

As these new tools become designed and generally available, the efficiency of these concepts may become acceptable. But this may not be all that likely because what is greatly underestimated is the complexity and volatility of the interrelationships of the elements of real-control information. Establishing an "integrated data base" with pointer arrays reflecting all these relationships would overwhelm any hardware power available in the foreseeable future. What is of even greater concern is the inflexibility of all this artificially created data structure.

It is an unfortunate likelihood that all these data-base concepts will never represent a satisfactory basis for storage organization because they are based on two very weak propositions. One is the use of the file-unit record as the basic element of data storage. This record concept, invented and implemented for use in the punched-card-driven computer environment, permeates all data-base concepts and associated programming languages. Though ideal only for the punch-card, batch-updated computer environment, it has been incorporated into all current data-base designs including those intended to support a real-time, random-accessed and updated computer service. With all the current trends toward real-time information processing, the weakness of the file, unit-record concept, especially as embodied in the concept of the "integrated data base," will clearly become apparent.

The other weak proposition supporting data-base concepts is that the real world of total corporate information flow can be defined, programmed, "integrated," and stored in interrecord pointer arrays, with or without dictionaries and data-base computers. The complexity of the processing of real-control information is grossly underestimated by the proponents of conventional data-base system concepts. Processed without computers, real-control information is used in decision-making processes that consist of some binary (yes/no) decisions mixed with many analog (judgmental/weighted) and political vectors of influence. Great flexibility is demanded of any data-base concept that is intended to be adapted to service this real-control information. To be at all practical, the user must be capable of being the base designer and modifier if any hope is to be entertained that the base can be practically adapted to the variety and complexity of real-control information and to the dictates of growth and change, the inevitable conditions encountered in any viable operation. Sterile, mappable patterns of information flow in a corporation or operation exist nowhere in reality.

In a vital, dynamic, growing corporation or operation, these patterns will be so varied and mercurial that they will continually defy and frustrate definition in programmed arrays and schemas. Only in older, more atrophied corporations would these patterns lend themselves to actual commitment to code in computer storage. Once put in place in the corporate body, the "integrated" data-base definition could well be the final step in a massive arterial blockage and result in a corporate cardiac arrest. The impossibility of redefining the total corporate data-base schema in a reasonable time could well prevent final restorative steps in saving a failing or troubled corporation.

10 Free Enterprise Computing Data-Base Theory

With Free Enterprise Computing, it is possible to let managment replace the schema, the pointer arrays, and the data-base dictionary. The result is that users are put in charge of data-base organization and management and are provided with the ability to manipulate the stored information with the power of electronic computing.

There is controversy today as to whether the Data Base Management System should reside in software logic or in hardware. Neither is correct. It should reside in the minds of management. It is their responsibility to control their operation. They must have the ability to establish their needed information relationships within their departments and with other departments and to upper management.

The invention of the concept of "decentralization" was the breakthrough that made the establishment of extremely large corporations possible. Without decentralization of autonomous control within corporate divisional management, General Motors would have failed due to an inability to manage because of its enormous size. Decentralization of control saved General Motors and became a standard of corporate organization and control throughout the world.

The same concept of decentralization of control is probably the only feasible means of computerizing the masses of data that comprise the real-control information that exists in all sizable operations. Only about 5 percent of all needed applications have been computerized with conventional programming techniques. To make computerizing the remaining 95 percent possible, decentralization of data-base management and Free Enterprise Computing concepts must be implemented.

Only by placing the establishment of inter- and intrabase relationships in the hands of user-management will it be possible to actually and properly create all the needed data bases. Only by placing control of the data base in the hands of the user-community is it possible to ensure the existance of a viable, dynamic data base that can automatically and quickly be adapted to the forces of change, the only dependable influence in all operations.

Management and data-processing personnel with line experience and respect for hardware and production-processing realities sense that the "integrated data base" and data-base concepts such as data-base dictionaries are simply too complex to be generally practical. The truth is that "rocket-scientist mentalities" are hard to find, expensive, and often impossible to keep. Yet this is the kind of talent needed to make the complex implementation of data-base systems work. Check the recent price tags on good, experienced, data-base managers.

Taken to the ultimate levels of development, data-base management concepts, as presently promoted by the data-base professionals, are highly questionable as to realistic attainability. If actually, extensively put in place, they could result in disasterous calcification of operational flexibilities, and high levels of serious incompetence are attainable.

Consider, instead, data-base evolution in a data-processing environment that supports and actively promotes Free Enterprise Computing concepts with real-time report processing being applied by the users in their own environment, which they fashion to service their most pressing information needs. Correct application priority is automatically set. Thus the greatest benefit is immediately obtained at the level that is most labor and material intensive and in the greatest need. The application is usually successful because the communication problems in translating the need into computer performance through computer professionals are eliminated when the users are the designers and implementers of the applications.

If oversights in design are made, the user-designer is directly responsible and must accept this responsibility. The users cannot complain that they misinterpreted the requirements of the application. This is of great importance when one considers that studies have shown that over 50 percent of the bugs in conventional applications are those associated with faulty requirement definition or interpretation. The user-designer approach does imply that the language used must allow convenient application correction and modification. Since it is possible to design real-time report-processing applications in a fraction of the time it takes to do conventional real-time application design, obviously application change can also be implemented in a fraction of time compared to conventional methods. In fact, most applications are not perfect as initially conceived and must be enhanced and adjusted with experience to obtain the full potential. In any case, all applications must be modified to meet the requirements of change in operations and policies.

As users are initially developing their report-processing applications, they have a natural tendency to restrict use and access to their immediate departments. This is a natural, human reaction when the information is new. Then as confidence in their application and information develops, they provide access (usually read only, no updating) to other departments. Then, as the value of interdepartmental input and information exchange becomes apparent, agreements are made to allow pertinent updating and access by outside users. Often, interdepartment application mergers are negotiated and consummated. This is encouraged by the central report-processing system coordination function. Thus a sharing of operational-level bases evolves naturally.

Also, as departmental bases more accurately reflect operational reality, the department managers develop upward-status reporting to their superiors from that information. The manager or departmental users design report generations for this status reporting to upper-management levels. Thus efficiency and reporting accuracy is greatly enhanced over the former primarily manual methods. A similar pattern of base and report-generation development repeats at each level, percolating up through the management structure.

Ultimately, then, an operation-wide, multilevel, computerized management-information system evolves that works and truly reflects reality. It works because it was developed from the bottom up by the users. True real-time computer power is implemented throughout the organization beginning at the most material- and labor-intensive level with the best possible set of implementation priorities and benefit realization. Management (users) control the application designs so they work and keep working because they will adjust their uses to meet new operational policies, directions, or growth potentials as they become necessary. This approach prevents the situation that occurs all too commonly where large, complex, conventionally structured systems calcify and even dictate operations policy instead of remaining passively utilitarian.

It is a fact that extensive report-processing systems are in existence and have been for years. Many of these are used in communication networks with more than a thousand display terminals and auxiliary devices on-line serving thousands of registered users. Some of these systems process millions of transactions involving hundreds of millions of lines of report data daily. The on-line data base on the larger of these systems consists of many millions of lines of report data. This is totally real-time information, which is easily updated. Large-scale services consisting of high volumes of real-time, random-access report processing with extensive real-time updating are supported. Even the largest systems enjoy average response times of less than a second per transaction.

The key to fast-response and high-processing-volume capacities in these services is that they use a modern data-base concept called the "Report Structured Data Base" (see chapter 18, figures 18-3 and 18-4). It is so named because the basic set of data stored and processed is called a *report*. It consists of a data set of usually less than 500 lines in length. The report data set is processed with general-purpose functions such as search, sort, or calculate. These functions are designed to program themselves automatically as they are executed. This base is conceptualized as data stored in electronic file cabinets in which each "drawer" constitutes the data associated with a given application, and the "packets" in the "drawer" are the reports. End-users can organize their information in this electronic-filing concept as conveniently and as understandably as they organize their information in their actual filing cabinets. This organization may be simple in the case of small bases or complex in relationships with index data logged in report-data context in the case of larger bases.

For instance, a reporting application may be set up to control work centers in a factory. Each report or packet in the drawer could be related to a given work center. Update conflicts are resolved at the report (packet) level. So, in a work-center status-reporting application in which one display is located in each work center to report job progress, one report per work center is a logical, simple, and practical data-base organization. Multiple retrieval processes such as display, search, sort, and calculate can be used on a given report while update is going on.

More complex arrangements can be made where the report is treated as a logical data set or "data bucket." For instance, a thousand reports (sets) may be set up for an inventory application. The three most random numbers (usually the last three) of the inventory item number will determine which report (set) the item record will be stored in. Thus a thousand logical entry points to the base are provided, and a thousand-to-one potential for momentary update conflicts to occur is created. Full item numbers are keyed into access screens, and report-generation functions interpret the item numbers to control access to the particular report (per the three numbers). The RPG function can also locate the specific inventory item in the report and present the required information.

Individual reports can be set up as indices that will give "drawer" and report identifiers (pointers) to create multiple paths of organized access to large bases. Thus even complex tabling concepts can be organized for efficient, large-base-access requirements.

The more complex report-organization techniques are used only in the larger-scale applications involving millions of line of information. However, the electronic-file-cabinet concept is simple enough that users can efficiently organize their information for real-time processing. Why not? They were capable of organizing file cabinets before computers and computer professionals came along.

Indeed, major report-processing systems exist today with real-time applications consisting of millions of lines of real-time processed and update information (see chapter 18, figure 18-6). These were designed and implemented by operations people. These people knew the application requirements and had access to a capable, user-oriented system that gave them the ability to be architects of their own systems and directors of computer power. They were not data-processing professionals. And these applications support high volumes of true, real-time updating with hundreds of displays on-line, in use performing hundreds of thousands of transactions with average response times of a second or less.

The Report Structured Data Base is not only simple to understand, it is efficient in delivering random-access report processing. The fact that the basic data set called the "report" is manipulated in storage means that the base is capable of sustaining high volumes of real-time updating without deteriorating in response time. This is possible because there is no conventional file-record organization involved that is susceptible to response deterioration due to record scattering in storage. This concept was developed as an evolution from conventional file-record-base concepts as they were found to be incapable of delivering high volumes of random-access report processing with extensive updating in real-time supported.

Functional interfaces are also provided to feed data collected in report context into conventional batch-processing systems or files (see chapter 18, figure 18-5). Also, functions are available to retrieve records from conventional files for entry into report data. Used in this way, the real-time, transaction-oriented, report-processing service becomes a powerful dimension of information processing and can be used with conventional batch processes as is advisable for efficiency in processing large quantities of records.

11 Distributed Processing: Cure or Cancer?

User disenchantment with centralized data processing in recent years has given impetus to concepts of computer utilization which would move data-processing resources into local user facilities. A whole new large-scale dimension of computer hardware and services marketing has been created. The buzz word for this multibillion-dollar marketing phenomenon is *distributed processing*. The term is very broad. It covers forms of data processing being done with "intelligent terminals" using microprocessors as well as the remote use of minicomputers as remote data-collection and data-processing systems. Sometimes we see the creation of complete remote data-processing centers where minicomputers are in use that might have been considered medium- to large-scale processors not too many years ago. It is in the latter case where distributed processing centers are allowed to become major service centers that dangerous evolutionary problems can be foreseen.

It is not commonly suggested that user disenchantment with centralized data processing is the primary motivating force behind development of the distributed-processing industry. Yet everyone with a feel for user unhappiness with centralized data-processing results has to see that dissatisfaction is indeed a primary impetus to the distributed-processing movement. The demand for distributed-processing service does not usually come from the centralized data-processing organization. It comes from the user organization, especially the user organization separated by a significant distance from the centralized DP shop. User dissatisfaction with central DP results is directly proportional to the distance between the user organization and central DP. Just as propinquity is a prime cause of infatuation, DP is most influenced by the nearest user. To put it another way, the closer the user is to DP, the greater will be the degree of satisfaction with DP results. So, of course, it is in the distant user organization that the distributed-processing revolution originates.

Sometimes, when enough of these nerve-end user organizations are set to jangling by the distributed-processing vendors, the centralized data-processing organization attempts to develop a cohesive corporatewide plan for distributed-processing implementation. Often this plan is late in being formed. This tardiness is natural because central DP is reluctant to see distributed processing implemented in any form whatsoever. Its introduction admits to weaknesses in the centralized data-processing service. It threatens the DP power structure, so there is a tendency to vacillate and procrastinate in the formation and enforcement of corporatewide distributed-processing policies. Meanwhile the distributed-processing marketers are not waiting. They have a broad-scale promotion going simultaneously against the end-user organizations with nifty offerings of relatively cheap state-of-the-art hardware with a variety of programming languages and packages all emphasizing "user-friendly" characteristics.

The concepts of distributed processing are being shrewdly marketed toward the end-users with concessions being made to centralized data processing. Depending on the political clout that a given centralized DP organization has, it will be given a corresponding degree of control over the establishment of the distributed-processing systems. From the corporate administrative viewpoint, which usually stresses uniform standards and coordinated planning, this seems to be a sound approach.

In acquiescing to the pressure from vendors and the users, much talk is made by the DP organization that distributed processing is needed to "unload the central processor." This idea is promoted in spite of the fact that raw processing power has been made abundantly available. The introduction of distributed processing into corporate data processing is normally proposed as a means of remote data-collection and application processing at the local facility with the idea that such data will be readily accessible and processed as elements of the common corporate data base.

In reality, this talk of the necessity of doing remote processing to unload the central processor and the idea that the data in the remote processor will be accessible as part of the corporate-data network is, for the most part, a DP face-saving front to distributing concepts. The real goal of the distributed-processing revolution is to get computer power into the hands of the end-user organizations.

Almost no data is actually transferred to the remote processors from the central processor. The only data that is sent into the central processor from the distributed processors is that which was summarized, cleaned, and sterilized by the remote-user group prior to submission or that data previously sent via data-collection sheets. The main use of the distributed processor is in the handling of local data-processing requirements. So, the bulk of the activity aims at solving the data-processing requirements that were ignored by centralized DP.

Sometimes applications operating in the central system that specifically pertain to a remote-user organization are converted to run on the remote distributed processor. The conversion to make the application run on the remote processor is often a mess because the conversion programmer usually has little or no minicomputer experience. In fact, if he or she were provided by central data processing, he or she probably has not had much experience at anything. The central DP department has no vested interest in making the conversion project a success.

Distributed processing may be better than the little processing that the remote-user organization used to get, but it is a far from satisfactory, long-range cure from the programming bottlenecks of centralized DP. The programming tumors, masses, and blockages of the centralized DP organization are carried throughout the corporate body with the dissemination of distributed-processing systems. The cells so dispersed are virulent and very dangerous because they land among end-users inexperienced in the pitfalls and opportunities of providing computer services.

Local line managers find themselves making highly technical decisions about which they are totally unqualified. They decide about such things as "system sizings," of "data-base schemas," things they never knew existed before. Because these are new experiences, they will surely make mostly wrong decisions, and poorly installed systems will certainly result. Restart, redirection, and abandonment are standard modes of operation in this amateur system management.

The minicomputer hardware offered is excellent for its size and cost, but it cannot match the economics of scale of the large-size centralized processors in efficient data handling. The Minicomputer Operating Systems (Executive) software is often limited in scope and power. The standard languages like COBOL and Fortran are much less capable than their equivalents in the large-scale-systems, and they suffer in use by the comparatively limited processing power of the minicomputers. The hardware-maintenance and software-utility libraries are limited in breadth, depth, and quality. The "user-friendly" languages provided are cosmetically attractive to the user community and on the surface would seem conducive to providing a Free Enterprise Computer service. But when stressed in high-volume use, the inefficiencies of generalization is revealed in weakness in the data-base structures. The control, monitor, and support utilities so essential to a viable system are usually dangerously lacking.

Probably the worst aspect of the whole distributed-processing concept is the fact that inexperience is a major characteristic of the implementors. Inexperienced users are expected to plan and oversee the installations, ensure adequate support and maintenance, and administer the systems. Small data-processing centers are being formed and manned with dangerous quantities of inexperienced personnel involved. If there is a shortage of programmers and systems people for large-scale systems, how can the source of personnel experienced in mini systems and the architecture of distributed systems be adequate?

It is really dangerous, this idea of distributed processing, especially if one considers the corporate considerations. Even if one can standardize the hardware installed (too often systems are installed piecemeal to solve local hot problems), programming standards become almost impossible to enforce.

It was hard enough to enforce such standards in the centralized systems. Data integrity and audit techniques are too often afterthoughts and extremely difficult to standardize and enforce throughout the dispersed centers.

Generally speaking, distributed-processing systems are not cost effective. They start out justified at purchase and installation costs but somehow seem to double in actual accomplishment. Hidden, unexpected costs creep in due to unforeseen system limitations and related compensating-equipment purchases. Studies generally show that the average business can do more on a larger central processor and do it for about half the cost of the distributed mini approach.

And, finally, because distributed processing does not support a true Free Enterprise Computing service, the end-user is still not allowed to be the architect of his or her own systems and director of his or her own computer power. Therefore, with time, will the structured bottlenecks not appear again as each of these small centers develops its unique bureaucracies? With small resources available in the distributed systems, the bottlenecks will be even more restricting.

Ultimately, then, the corporate body will be riddled with the same malignant cells that precipitated the rush to distributed processing. The effect could be terminal for corporations or operations who go too far down this path.

12 Free Enterprise Report Processing instead of Distributed Processing

Free Enterprise report processing conducted in large-scale, centralized processors can satisfy all the basic desires that cause users to go to distributed processing. It satisfies their needs at each level of service required and does so in a system-safe, controlled, properly supported environment. At the same time corporate systems and resources can be properly mixed in to the report-processing service, either appropriately feeding the service from structured system records or receiving appropriate information from it.

At first, in new applications, user independence can be provided for parochial report-processing services. Data-base securities can be set at appropriate levels to provide the freedom to develop the control information processing needed at the divisional offices and shops. These walls can be built as high and tight as is needed or deemed necessary by the related departmental authority to ensure local autonomy over their portion of the system use. A report-processing system coordination function that is supportive of a service that encourages a Free Enterprise environment for the users will be sensitive to the needs of the remote user for parochial autonomy. This is especially important in the beginning phases of reporting development. The end-user management must have the authority to decide where to establish reporting and with what priorities. The initial goal is to establish computerized reporting at the working level, the most labor- and material-intensive level of the operation. As remote operational management becomes satisfied and confident that local reporting is accurately reflecting reality in a timely manner, they can decide to use this information as input to upward-reporting processes. So, with this approach, divisional management controls not only policy but also the flow of information. This is correct and in keeping with modern concepts of decentralized corporate management.

When the end-users in the many remote operations design their own report-processing applications many important benefits are obtained. One of the most important is savings in application-programming costs. These reporting applications are implemented in a fraction of the time over alternate methods. Of course, it is important to recognize that this is real-time application design with real-time updating capabilities being implemented. This is the trickiest and most time-consuming sort of programming when conventional languages are used.

When a report-processing language is used, language as well as hardware standardization is automatic. The benefits of the "user-friendly" report-processing system are so obvious that the language, the data-base structure, and the hardware it operates on are all automatically accepted. Comparable alternatives of similar substance and capability do not exist. Standardization is automatically accepted as far as the user-community is concerned.

One of the greatest benefits obtained from the use of Free Enterprise report-processing concepts as an alternative to conventional distributed-processing concepts is the fact that the users are the architects of each of these myriad applications. With this highly distributed ability to conveniently mold computer power, the decentralized systems of reporting are adjusted by local management as required to meet the requirements of change, growth, and corporate policy directions. People then are not only in charge of policy change, they can adapt computer power to these changes in the way and on a schedule that perfectly suits the specific local operation.

If the operation is large enough to justify the use of multiple large-scale processors, these can be placed in strategic locations to serve different geographic areas. Remote plants can use concentrators to which their terminals are connectd. The concentrators then use a single high-speed communication line connected to nearest area central processors. These area processors are then linked together with high-speed data lines. Thus a powerful network of computer power is made possible with the best economies of scale relative to processor and communications resources.

Ultimately, corporatewide computerization of information is then a possibility. It begins at the bottom in the most work-intensive areas and percolates its way up through the management levels. Eventually, a corporatewide base of computerized real-control information is in place, and it works. It reflects reality on a timely basis. And, most important, it changes to meet new corporate directions. This represents the eptiome of computer use for information processing. It is a use of computers as it has always seemed they should be used, as a convenient, adaptive extension of the human mind.

13 Implications for Data Processing

But how should the data-processing department properly view the concept of Free Enterprise Computing? From the past experience of Free Enterprise report processing's being implemented in numerous, major operating environments, the record indicates that it is an unsettling experience, to say the least. All DP professionals do not oppose this concept, but many do. It seems that the more the DP professionals are indoctrinated in integrated data-base philosophies, the more skeptical and resistant they are to the idea that end-users can be the effective architects of their own systems. The intensive technical indoctrination they have received seems to confuse their ability to accept the evolutionary nature and simplicity inherent in decentralized, Free Enterprise Computing concepts.

The more myopic and self-centered of the DP professionals even see a threat to job security in the appearance of Free Enterprise Computing concepts. In actuality, this is a totally unfounded fear. Even in operations in which these concepts have been in evolutionary use for over ten years, the data-processing department is still large and still possesses long backlogs of conventional, structured application development to be done. They are still overworked and are still trying to hire system planners and programmers and are experiencing the same frustrations in that regard as the rest of the data-processing industry. What is totally underestimated by everyone is the amount of information processing in the world that remains to be computerized.

Some data-processing departments have established large Free Enterprise Computing services as part of their operations and have integrated this service with conventional structured systems very successfully. These DP departments have learned to not only coexist with Free Enterprise Computing services but have become supportive and capable of using such services as advisable in their own operations. They use report processing for administrative control of the operation of their computer centers and their projects and as a prototyping aid to improve the efficiency of their conventional software-design processes.

The convenient flexibility of the report-processing environment provides not only a medium for specification development, it also serves to test the concepts of major real-time structured systems on a small scale prior to investing the major programming effort. This gives added insurance that the structured program will be successful because a smaller-scale simulation with the real-time report-processing service creates a means of illustrating the ultimate, structured, real-time product.

The introduction of Free Enterprise Computing into the information-processing environment does not threaten data processing. In fact, instead it can compliment and even strengthen data processing's role. A major role is played by the data-processing professional in providing the system-hardware capacity to support the Free Enterprise Computing service in conjunction with the conventional software systems. Often this is done in the same computer or at least in the same center. Installation and maintenance of the communications networks, terminals, auxiliary devices and peripherals are all essential roles. Also, many of the report-processing applications will be integrated, or they will evolve into some relationship with the existing conventional systems. Examples of these relationships are: using report processing as a data-collection media for batch updating of conventional systems; extracting records from the conventional systems to report processing for convenient, programmerless manipulation; or passing closed report-processing records to conventional storage media for large-scale history retention and processing.

Indeed, the role of the data-processing department is not threatened. It is made into a more powerful, responsive resource. By delivering a sound, Free Enterprise Computing service to the large enthusiastically receptive user-community, the data-processing department will enjoy a new image of value and appreciation that may not have often been theirs in the past.

If they lead the way, promote and are supportive of these concepts, they will be given credit for the valuable contribution the introduction of Free Enterprise Computing will make in the operation. If they are less than enthusiastically supportive or even openly hostile to the concepts, they may find themselves supporting very unwise positions.

Free Enterprise Computing is an idea whose time has come. Freedom has always proven to be a powerful motivational force, and it is no less true when associated with Free Enterprise Computing. This is virtually an irresistible force that can be only temporarily slowed in its progress by an intransigent data-processing department. Those who go with it, support it, and use it will enjoy the challenge and opportunity and will be rewarded according to the effectiveness with which they employ it.

So data processing must not merely concern itself with a self-seeking preservation of a conventional programming status quo. The fact that this is not a tenable position is evident throughout the industry. Instead, the view that serves the corporation or operation best must prevail. The 95 percent of the information of the world that comprises the real-control information in all operations waits to be computerized.

This computerization would require armies of real-time systems analyst and programming talent if conventional computerization methods are to be used. Given the fact that real-control information is too unique, mercurial, and volatile to be computerized with conventional programming methods, only user-oriented concepts such as Free Enterprise Computing can make automation of this infomation possible. To block the computerization of an operation's real-control information is to block an opportunity for productivity improvement of major significance. The data-processing department that resists the computerization of real-control information does no service but rather a serious disservice to the operation. Conversely, to aid in such computerization, to lead the way, is to provide a service of great importance and benefit to the operation.

Report-Processing Systems as Application Design Languages

A system that is capable of supporting a Free Enterprise Computing environment is implicitly a very efficient application design language. If such a system is treated by programmers as an application design language, significant improvements in application design efficiency are attained. Experience with such systems has clearly demonstrated that applications can be generated in one-fifth the time or less using report-processing systems than could be done with conventional languages and data-base techniques. Application design efficiencies are especially noteworthy when the applications are more complex than simple retrieval report generators. Efficiencies are especially noteworthy where the applications to be designed involve a real-time transaction orientation with extensive real-time updating involved.

There are a number of reasons why this application design efficiency is possible:

Functions are powerful instructions. The report-processing functions represent powerful instructions. They provide significant leverage in the design process.

Data-base support is greatly simplified. The convenience and flexibility of the report structured data-base facilitates rapid data-base organization and modification.

Recovery and history design is provided. The standard, fast, reliable recovery and history-production methods of report-processing systems are used, and thereby a complex design burden is greatly simplified.

System monitors enhance application design efficiencies. The transactional system monitors available through the coordination function allow extensive efficiency measurements. When these monitors and

measurements are properly used, they can greatly improve design effectiveness and application efficiencies.

Interactive design processes are fast. Report-processing systems support interactive application design at both the functional and report-
generator level. As soon as data bases are formed, they can be tested using the manually executed functions of the report-processing system.
Since the functions are also used as instructions in RPG design, the
statements can be immediately, interactively tested as they are written.
Resulting diagnostics are instantly provided. Debug is very fast.

These application design efficiencies are also attained when the user is the
application designer. Of course, the user has the added advantage of knowing what the problem to be solved is. So the definition of the application
between the user and the designer is greatly minimized.

However, in cases in which an application is extensive and involves
multiple parts of the operation across significant different departments, the
data-processing department will often assume overall responsibility for the
application design. Then all the conventional disciplines of application
specification and design would be brought into effect. Even then, the efficiencies inherent in report-processing systems, when used as an application
language, will provide efficiency improvements of five to one or better over
conventional methodologies.

Developing Data-Processing Personnel for Report-Processing
Application Design

It is a significant fact that the more sophisticated and experienced a data-
processing person is in conventional methodologies, the less likely it is that
such a person will be comfortable or even effective when trained to do
report-processing system application design. This is especially true for the
DP person steeped in conventional transaction-processor technologies and
especially in data-base system-management philosophies. Such a person has
great problems in conceiving how the user-oriented, simplistic concepts of
report processing could be effective in any complex application design. The
report-structured data-base concepts also give such a person great problems
of understanding as compared to the familiar file-records concepts conventionally used in data-base management systems.

Another type of data-processing person who has problems being trained
to be an effective report-processing system application designer is one
whose background is primarily COBOL or batch-processing oriented. Not
only does such a person have problems making a transition from thinking

of data bases as consisting of files and records instead of reports, such a person also has problems with a real-time transaction orientation in processing. Real-time updating of data is especially difficult to comprehend for such batch-experienced personnel. They tend to think in terms of mass updating and massive data analysis rather than having an orientation to real-time problem solving using real-control information transactionally. When learning something new, they always tend to correlate the new methods to those with which they are familiar. The extensive DP background is not necessarily a great asset in learning the new user-oriented concepts of evolutionary report-processing application design.

The simple, user-oriented language of systems capable of supporting Free Enterprise Computing such as the report-processing systems make it possible to tap new sources for developing application design talent, mainly from the user community where the operations environment is an excellent source of talent. It may be faster and easier and more effective to train a bright, innovative person from the operations environment in report-processing applications design procedures than it is to retrain a sophisticated, highly experienced data-processing person. The key to this fact is the simplicity of the language. The user's operational experience is an added plus.

The sophistication of the DP-experienced designer will tend to over-complicate the applications design. The user-trained designer will tend to simplify the design. This is especially apparent in the design of input-edit techniques. The DP-experienced designer will edit to the extreme, thereby greatly adding unnecessarily to the overhead of the system. The user-experienced designer will use minimal edits, and the design flexibility of the report-processing system will let edits be appropriately added quickly as their needs are proven in application testing and actual use. The DP-experienced designer will tend to overspecify and predefine all considerations. The user-experienced designer will tend to prespecify less and use a more evolutionary design approach. The DP-experienced designer will tend to use the read line, write line (read a record and write a record), if, and GO TO logic to the exclusion of the more powerful report-processing functions. The user-experienced designer will go to read line and write line only after the potentials of the more powerful and efficient report-processing functions have been exhausted. The user-experienced designer will thereby be much more efficient and effective in related learning process as well as in accomplishing efficient application designs in an evolutionary manner.

The implications of these facts are very significant. When the language is easy to use, it is also easy to teach. Therefore, the people who are experienced in operations realities and who are familiar with the problems to be solved can best be trained to be application designers. The programmer-talent bottleneck can be overcome by turning bright users into application designers.

14 Auditing Report-Processing Services

Just as real-time report-processing concepts create problems of understanding and management for conventional data-processing organizations, the corporate auditors also sometimes have problems when they try to apply conventional auditing procedures to this volatile reporting environment.

When the data base is constantly changing in a real-time reflection of actual conditions of the moment in the operations, it is no longer an acceptable procedure to "stop the world and count the beans." Auditing must now learn to "count the beans while someone is shaking the jar." In others words, the operation should not be stopped to take an inventory check. Instead, cyclical-sampling techniques should be used to periodically check inventory validities. Only if the inventory samples show a potentially deviant inventory should an operation be halted for more complete physical inventories.

Cyclical-sampling methods, instead of periodic operation stopage with total physical inventorying, are much more efficient, effective, and less disruptive to the operations. The cyclical testing on a frequent, periodic basis will detect problems at an earlier stage before serious inventory discrepancies develop. The operation that retains effective inventory control is not unnecessarily interrupted while the operation that tends to use ineffective inventory-control techniques is promptly caught at an early stage of deviation before serious problems develop.

Today computerized real-time inventory reporting is not very common in most operations. This is real-control information, which, as this book has pointed out, has not until now been adaptable to computer control. However, as these volatile inventories become more and more computerized, it will become more and more important for auditing to understand how to deal with the changing information as reflected in these bases.

New understanding is not only necessary in dealing with real-time inventory data bases, but the new movement of application design into the user-community has very important implications for computer-audit policies and procedures. No longer is application design funneled through the neatly grouped and tightly disciplined data-processing department that helped in making the computer audit capable of being a procedure of some precision and finite dimensions.

In a properly implemented Free-Enterprise computer environment, application design power and authority is disseminated throughout the user-community. Not only is application design not neatly coralled in the data-processing department but the real-time nature of applications design associated with Free-Enterprise Computing creates an enormous potential for convenient and continuous application change. Entire new reporting applications are conceived and implemented in days. Changes are frequently accomplished in hours or minutes. Clearly, this can be traumatic for a computer-audit function that conventionally saw all computerization neatly specified in advance and a common design process taking many months. The new user-oriented computer environment is clearly decentralized and volatile.

If auditors attempt to enforce the same audit procedures on Free Enterprise Computing services as they used on conventional applications systems designs, they will have serious, negative petrifying effects. Such obsolete methods will greatly distract from the potentials of effective real-time control and productivity of these services.

What auditing must clearly recognize is the fact that the computer is simply a media. In the Free Enterprise Computing environment, the computer has become a tool that can be directly used and molded to applications by users in the operations. The control information is still control information as it was before it was computerized. It is simply more productively processed because it can be computerized.

User-management must be in charge of the use of this medium and must be designated directly responsible for its use. The audits then are basically the same audits that would have been enforced on this information regardless of the media. No mystique should develop because it suddenly is processed in a computer instead of on paper.

The volatile nature of Free Enterprise Computing applications imply that the best media for documenting the applications is on the computer. Paper documentation would be too inflexible. The documentation must be as easily changeable as the application itself. Often the applications can be self-documenting. Prespecification is usually useless and self-defeating. The applications can be designed in less time than it would take to prespecify these applications. As the design solidifies with actual use, documentation should be developed to ensure a transition with personnel turnover. Over-decumentation that could prevent convenient application adaptation should not be required.

Auditing should look for a reasonable level of documentation on Free Enterprise Computing applications that indicate that the operations management has control of these developments. Reliance on management responsibility is the key to an effective control.

The use of adequate and proper security techniques in a Free Enterprise Computing environment should be a primary concern of the auditors. Assuming that a user-oriented system is selected that has sufficient security techniques available, auditing should validate that they are being adequately used. They should be documented in the policies and guidelines available to the user-community, and auditing should assure the proper enforcement of these policies through an effective system-coordination function.

However, the primary responsibility for security must rest with the managers of the application designers and data-base owners. Absolute and total security is an impossibility. It cannot be achieved by hardware or systems technology. It must remain management's responsibility to ensure an adequate security for their use and base accesses. They are on the firing line. They know the sensitivity of their applications and data. They must be aware of the security techniques that are possible and determine the adequacy of these techniques relative to their applications. A knowledgeable, supportive coordination service is a key to disseminating knowledge of security methods and encouragement of their effective use through user-management.

When real-control information was contained in the paper media and in desks and file cabinets, management was assumed to be clearly capable of security management related to such information. The same is true when the computer becomes the media. User-management that is capable of controlling application development can also determine adequacies of security for computerized real-control information. The new media should not promote new security paranoia simply because a computer is involved.

Promotion of proper security attitudes among the users is an important facet of effective application development and use. Need to know is primary in computer security too. Dissemination of security keys to only qualified personnel is an obvious discipline. The transaction logging process of the selected user-oriented system is a key factor in promoting proper attitudes that only proper activites are wise will more likely prevail. The logging records obviously are of immense importance in an evidential and use-analysis sense. Auditing must learn the potentials of log analysis and effective uses of the related techniques to ensure that the coordination functions properly administer them.

It is important for significant inventory-control applications to have audit trails developed with them. These trails consist of a continuous record of the adds and deletes from the inventories. They are used to aid in inventory correction where current records become out of synchronization with reality. Auditors should encourage the use of such audit trails on important inventory applications.

One of the most important contributions auditors can make to an operation is to urge and support the development of a Free Enterprise computer-service environment, thereby affecting great productivity improvements. Often this will involve positively influencing the conventional data-processing department to be supportive of user-oriented services.

Auditors should also stress the enforcement of an effective coordination function. Auditing should become familiar with the concepts of creating a Free Enterprise Computing service environment and the tools of coordination that make that environment most effective. By making sure that the coordination of functions is properly administered and that all the tools are being properly used, auditing can make an enormous contribution to the overall effective use of computers in the operation.

15 Purchase Considerations for User-Oriented Software Systems

The trend to user-oriented software systems is clearly visible. The industry's periodicals are full of articles calling for attention to the enormous demand for applications to be computerized and the dangerous shortage of systems analysts and programmers to develop them. They have clearly identified the fact that large portions of the current programming staffs are involved in maintenance programming on existing applications. Users and proposals for new applications are stacked up in long queues waiting for their share of the scarce system-analyst and programming resources. The lack of adequate quantities of data-processing personnel has been called a worldwide crisis.

The need to improve productivity in all operations creates an enormous demand to apply computers, and the shortage of data-processing professionals constitutes a severe bottleneck to efficiency improvement. Computer power gets cheaper and inversely more plentiful, but the users cannot get at it. The capacity of educational institutions to fill this data-processing gap with computer professionals is severly limited because professors who have data-processing and system-design knowledge are attracted to the high salaries paid by industry for such talent and skills.

Obviously, a great need exists for systems that allow users to be architects of their own computer applications. Only by giving the users the ability to mold computer power to their needs can the conventional programmer crisis be overcome. Most of the system vendors recognize this need and are announcing software systems that are "user friendly." On the surface, many of these systems sound wonderful and are very attractive to the user-community. However, the user-friendly software system marketplace is a field of many newcomers, and many of these offerings lack important features. Some of these systems are indeed user friendly; some, however, could not be called "friend."

For instance, "relational" systems are now heavily promoted as supportive of end-user application design. However, a certain amount of end-user confusion is understandable when he or she is faced with a system that can supposedly be related to but requires extensive, complex articles to define what *relational* means. Not only is this system title confusing but when its internal architecture is described as consisting of "tuples," "cardinality," "degrees," "domains," "normal form 1,2,3," "homogeneous columns," and so on, one has to wonder whether its primary appeal is still not to the end-user but rather to the data-processing establishment.

71

Even if a particular system seems user friendly, in deciding which of these systems will do a good job, it is important to look beyond the user cosmetics of these systems. Besides ease of use, it is important that a system is chosen with adequate capacity, capabilities, reliability, and support facilities. It is important not to underestimate the demand that will be encountered once such a capability is demonstrated and offered in a particular operation. The system will almost surely become a major utilitarian service in the operation. The system chosen therefore must be capable of meeting this challenge satisfactorily since it is very difficult to change systems later in the growth cycle.

The choice of a user-oriented system is probably the most important computer decision that an organization will ever make. Because experience with these kinds of systems is uncommon, there is a tendency on the part of data-processing professionals as well as the users to underestimate the potentials of this kind of service. Clearly, the potential is enormous. Ultimately, 95 percent of the computer cycles of the world will be dedicated to the processing of user-developed and user-controlled applications. The full potentials of computer utilization have just been scratched. Given these facts, obviously, the choice of user-oriented system assumes unusual significance.

These are some of the considerations that are essential to the selection process of a user-oriented computer system that could provide a satisfactory Free Enterprise Computing service.

Growth Potential

Proper system selection requires the choice of a vendor and computer system that can not only do current applications but can grow with a company or operation. There are two aspects of this growth. One relates to computer power and system hardware expandability. The other relates to software-system growth. The choice of a vendor with a substantial history of major system marketing and support goes without saying. Reliability of product and its support is essential.

The initial hardware selection can be made on a scale that is suitable for the beginning growth phase. But it is imperative that the hardware comes from a line that is expandable to a large-scale system. Certainly, as the Free Enterprise Computer service grows, hardware capacities will have to be added to support it. So a system should be chosen that has sufficient processing muscle and expandability to multiprocessor power. Unless the organization is a very small operation with little growth potential, it should steer clear of the micro or minisystem vendors of user-friendly systems. It may not be possible to add the computer power ultimately needed. Conversions among different families of hardware with the same vendor is difficult enough. If the vendor does not have the additional power when the organization needs it, both systems and vendors will have to be changed.

The software system must be operable on higher-powered configurations of the system hardware without reprogramming. This is called *upward software compatibility.* User-oriented real-time systems are not easy to reprogram, so the software system chosen should run all the way up the hardware line selected.

Software systems capable of supporting Free Enterprise Computing need extensive use to get all the bugs out and develop to full competence. Thus an extensive history of use is essential. These systems are not designed to be used just one way. Many functional capabilities are provided with many options. These must all be exercized in all possible ways in mixed-service environments to ensure they all operate and are bug free. It is almost impossible to simulate a Free Enterprise user-community in operation on a computer system. So final debugging of such a system can be done only in the real-world mix of high-volume, random-access, real-time production processing. Evidence of this high-volume use is an essential qualification criteria for the choice of a suitable Free Enterprise Computing system.

It is important to study system and hardware specifications in the selection process, but demonstrable capabilities are equally important. Test drives by purchasing end-users are essential in choosing user-oriented systems. Demonstrations of the system's capacity to process in large volumes are imperative. Contact with the users of the proposed system who have a large user-oriented service in existence is very helpful. This should consist of at least 500 terminals on-line with access to a data base of over one billion characters. This must be a data-base capable of being totally, randomly updated in real-time.

Insistence on demonstrable, large-volume-processing capacities is especially necessary with the user-oriented system. Because this service involves the ability to support a random-access processing service as well as high volumes of real-time updating, a great deal of system efficiency is implicit in the acceptable system design. Systems based on obsolete file concepts will not be capable of handling the high volumes. It is imperative that system inefficiencies be detected before the system becomes prematurely saturated. Large-scale, existant user-communities yield important proofs of system capacities and efficiencies.

The need to have evidence of high volumes of real-time data updating must be stressed to the vendor. At least 10 percent of the on line base should be updated on a given day. This would be minimally characteristic of a true, real-time data base consisting of volatile control information. There are numerous report-generating systems on the market. They are called *RPG systems* or *Report Writers.* Many of these are capable only of convenient data formating and calculations in a retrieval-only mode of operation. If the files are batch updated and only retrieved in real-time, the system is not a true real-time system. It will not be capable of processing real-control information with up-to-the-minute reflections of current activities. Convenient data formating is not the same as the processing of real-control information and system efficiency is a key factor in the successful product design.

Functional Comparison

One of the first comparisons usually made in the evaluation of user-oriented systems is of the functional processing capabilities. Too often it is the primary consideration in system choice. In reality, it is only a cosmetic consideration. Many of the other considerations in this section are of much greater importance. Almost all systems offer the basic processes of search, sort, and print, and they offer a computational capability for performing arithmetic on numeric data. Not all systems, however, offer an ability to determine match or non-match characteristics between data sets. A date-manipulation and analysis function is a real plus, especially when handling time-sensitive real-control information. Functions that allow the locating or changing of strings of characters, words, names, titles, and so on within textual data are also very helpful.

Real-time-updating capability is, of course, a mandatory functional characteristic of the acceptable user-oriented system. Important efficiencies can be obtained if mass updating functions are provided. For instance, functions that can extract items with a common characteristic such as a status code or date into a collected data set on the basis of search or match processes are very desirable. The updates can then be entered into the collected set instead of into their normal locations. Then when all updates to the collected data set are done, the collected data is blended back into the master data sets. Quick mass updating of common items in this manner can be very efficient as compared to manual, single-item-updating processes.

By far the most important functional characteristic to evaluate is ease of use. Without real ease of use, how can end-users become molders of computer power? This is a very difficult comparison factor to assess, especially in measurable terms. This cannot be determined from reading the sales literature or system specifications. There is really only one way to determine ease of use, which is by extensive, live demonstrations. Ideally, these tests should be conducted with some real data used by the organization. A simple application should be set up to see how easy the language is to use.

Many of the so-called user-friendly systems being offered tout what they call "programming the system with English-like statements." An example might be an instruction to "find all the inventory items that are over one month old." On the surface, that sounds like a user-oriented method of functional specification. However, in reality there is much more symantic precision involved than is at first apparent. The statement must be quite precise. Since the statement can be worded differently by different users, and most systems will not tolerate much deviation from the system-prescribed terms and form.

Menu-oriented systems are also available. This approach assumes that all the choices that could possibly be conceived of for a particular information-processing system have been previously cataloged. This method is self-limiting and is not flexible enough for real-world processing within the unique characteristics of a particular operational environment.

Some of the easiest functional-control methods are those by which parameters for processing are submitted in the context of the data being accessed. For instance, if a date is to be searched for, it is submitted in a control mask showing the header from the date field of the data to be searched. The reason this technique is so easy to use is that the user's own data become the language of programming, or the functional parameter. Obviously, this is ideal if the user designs the format of his or her own data. By defining the form of the data base, the user is creating the parameters of the (see chapter 18, figures 18-1 and 18-2) system language. How can the user fail to understand this language since it is his or her own? Use of this technique is one of the primary reasons for the success of the report-processing class of systems in delivering Free Enterprise Computing concepts.

History of Support

System support is of course an essential consideration in the choice of a user-oriented computer system. Support must cover both the hardware and the software of the system. The nature and costs of the support must be spelled out in the contractual agreement. But even more important, the quality of this support should be verifiable as a history of satisfaction with the existing user-community.

A real-time, Free Enterprise Computing service becomes an extremely important, utilitarian function in an operational environment. This is the processing of real-control information. It is implicit then that the support be prompt and effective. Downtime of the service can have severe impacts if they are lengthy. It is advisable to consider what outages could do to the operation. If lengthy outages occur, some insurance in the form of intelligent terminals with diskettes for transaction collecting in crucial control areas may be advisable. For most operations, interim paper processing will serve to bring the users through a lengthy outage. An acceptable system will have rapid recovery procedures to resolve minor interruptions. The period of catch up after a system outage is a critical test of system capacities. The catch-up load far exceeds the normal waves of demand encountered in average system processing.

Security Techniques

In the choice of a user-oriented system, the security techniques provided are a very important consideration. Such a system must allow individual-user sign-on as an essential factor of security clearance. People must be controlled as individual users. Generally, the distribution of a common sign-on greatly obscures the ability to relate a given user to a given task and should be avoided. When users know that the things they do on a system are done in their own names, a better attitude toward security is fostered. They should also have an option to have a password to enter with their names to prevent its use by others. They should have the right to use and alter this password at their discretion. Thus use of their own names and the protection thereof is primarily their responsibility.

The selected system must have the ability to discriminate functional abilities to specific users. It should be possible to turn on or off each functional ability that the system offers for each individual user. This assures that each user has the functional processing skills appropriate to his or her particular position. It also makes it possible to turn on functional powers for users when they have developed the skills to handle them effectively. For instance, the ability to execute report generators may be given to the lowest clerical function because the only logic that has been designed into the report generator is the logic that can be performed by its execution. The more general-purpose functions such as search, sort, and calculate could be allowed for aministrative users once they have been trained in these basic skills. If a particular person proved to be unskilled or persistently abusive with a certain function, its accessibility could be turned off for that user until appropriate remedial or disciplinary steps had been taken.

The functional power to perform higher-level skills such as designing report generators would also be turned on once skill levels were verified. Certain powers would be restricted to certain system-support personnel. For instance, the ability to turn on new reporting applications would be restricted to the coordination function, thus ensuring an operable planning process for total system-resource consumption.

The ability to perform system-support functions such as system initializations, history production, and system recovery in case of failure would be reserved for the central-system operators and support personnel. The system-support programmers must have access to the conventional-system compilers and assemblers and diagnostic routines for internal system maintenance. Of course, the end-users should be restricted from such powers due to their limited skill levels. The knowledge in the user-community that functional powers can be turned off if abused provides a valuable stimulus to sound security attitudes.

When a user signs on, that user should be placed in the data area used most. Sign-on should not be a license for total base accessibility. Access to the data related to the user's job is all the user should have access to. With password knowledge and an allowed ability to switch data areas, movement within the base may be permitted. For a given user, it may be appropriate that the user be locked into a certain data area. This capability should exist.

Access to a data area should be capable of being set at a read-only mode of operation (no updating allowed). Even if read and write (look and update) capability is allowed in a certain data area, it must also be possible to set update password protection at the specific data-subset level. Also, with access to an area of data, it should be possible to discriminate where necessary as to which fields (columns) of data can be seen in display or processing.

Use of password protection to control data access and updating is a useful technique but it is really effective only from a security standpoint if the passwords are changed frequently. This should be encouraged. The basic responsibility for password determination and dissemination is the user-owner's. Neither data-processing personnel nor the system coordinator should assume this responsibility. The determination of the level of security sensitivity and the need to modify or establish security methods must be the responsibility of user-management.

In the case of very security-sensitive information such as personnel information, cost files, or schedules, simple password-security methods are not adequate. It should be possible to protect access to such sensitive data areas with more complex algorithmic methods. For example, a report generator could be used to set up complex security tests that would have to be cleared, at which time, access to the sensitive area would be provided. Also, it is desirable that the security-clearance report generator be restricted to a specific signed-on user or users and to a restricted station or stations. By using the RPG language to develop clearance schemes, it becomes possible for users to create their own complex security systems, thereby, again, reinforcing their responsibility for the security control of their own information.

Key to effective security control and an absolute requirement of the user-oriented system is effective transaction records. User-community knowledge that such a record is constantly being maintained on their activity is a very strong deterrent to inappropriate actions. The needed contents of such transaction records are discussed in the selection-criteria section,

"Tools for System Coordination." Of course, to make these transaction records effective in security control, they must be accessible and processed selectively in real-time and through batch-summary analysis. They must truly qualify as real-control information in the clearest sense.

Certain kinds of information require that a trail of actual data entries be retained for auditing purposes. This capability would be too great an overhead burden for all reporting applications, but it is usually advisable in such cases as inventory-control applications. To monitor inventory accurately, a record of additions and deletions from inventory is needed as well as a record of basic transactional statistics. In such applications, access for updating the base is allowed only through the specific logic of report generators, and that logic will also record the needed audit data.

Adequate security techniques are obviously essential. Thus in a real-time system, establishing and modifying security controls must be accomplished in real-time. These security controls include user registration, functional switchability, password change, and terminal registration and deregistration. These controls do exist in some of the real-time systems on the market today and buyers can obtain adequate security measures for user-oriented computer services.

Education and Documentation

Complete and thorough system documentation is especially critical to a user-oriented system. The education and tutorial aids must be aimed at and be effective at the end-user interface. On-line self-teaching aids can provide great savings in training costs as well as in documentation purchasers. Also, many systems are now being sold as "unbundled" products in which hardware, education, and documentation are all sold as separately priced items. In these products, obviously, on-line documentation and tutorials that are part of the system rental charge are very important. Also, the decentralized availability of on-line references and tutorials at the display terminals provide access to the needed information at the point of use at the time it is needed.

In performing the user-oriented processing, often a question of technique will occur or a reminder will be needed. When the system makes this help available on request at the terminal, it represents a real plus. Even better is a system that senses the type of error that the user is encountering and, when help is requested, places the user automatically into the section of the tutorial information that pertains to the error.

Another form of education is that provided by the new media of video cassette. These are usually supplemented with a course guide that, combined with the audio-visual presentations make a very effective learning experience. This also has the advantage of reusability, transportability, and decentralized group teaching that you can schedule. This lets you avoid the expenses and inconveniences of sending students to vendor-provided classes.

Automatic History Production

Historical data accessibility is a necessary complement to general-purpose information processing. This process is an essential part of the system. The process of historical data retention must be automatic as far as the end-user is concerned. A system that requires a separate, specific act by the end-user to save his or her portion of the data base for historical access is unacceptable. History retention is necessary to the recovery systems, and therefore, there is usually little problem in using this as a source of automatic history retention. If history retention is not a by-product of general system-support procedures, it may be a reflection of the quality of the recovery system. This aspect should be checked out carefully.

The requirement of history is often hard to predict. Daily copies of the on-line data should be made to magnetic tape. The retention of these tapes in a library will provide access to historical versions of the data when required. The depth of the history will depend on the quantity of tapes retained. Processes must be available to retrieve the data by reading the data from the selected history tape and copying it into the current, on-line base.

The system that cannot demonstrate a complete historical data philosophy and functional processes of historical-data production and accessibility must be considered an incomplete system. Such a lack is probably indicative of a system that is lacking an in-depth, real-world exposure and experience of use. Historical-data retention and accessibility is an absolute essential in a viable, production-information-processing system.

The Communication System

Flexibility and ease of maintenance are two essential considerations in evaluating the communication capabilities of the system. The communications equipment, the displays and auxiliary devices are subject to movement and expansion because of their direct involvement in the end-user environment. Therefore, it is essential that the configuration parameters of the communication system be capable of being established and controlled in real-time while the system is running. This may not seem very important in the embryonic stages of system implementation, but as the system grows in scope and utilitarian importance, system shut-down to adjust communication definitions becomes less tolerable. In addition, real-time configuration and adjustment of the parameters is characteristic of a soundly designed system. It should be able to accommodate real-time updating and adjustment of its system parameters. Such flexibility also means a display or device can be quickly disabled from system use in case of security violations or hardware problems.

The maintenance aids for the communication system provided as part of the package should be examined. They should provide real-time communication-system status monitoring. Error-characteristic collection should also be provided. Real-time visibility as to who is on-line, on which display, and doing what are important system-management aids. Again these capabilities become more important as the system grows in size to high levels of use. Without these visibilities, the distributed communications network becomes a nightmare of guesswork to manage and maintain as use patterns change and line and device qualities fluctuate.

Display Terminals

The choice of the software system will determine the choice of the display terminals. The systems are usually associated with a certain family of terminals and auxiliary devices. Clarity of character presentation is, of course, a prime concern to minimize eye strain in display use. The display size must be at least twenty-four lines by eighty characters in width. Full-screen data rolling or scrolling will be a feature of the acceptable system, and the larger the screen, the more effective this function is. The quieter display or device is more desirable in the office environment. The modern displays do not require fan cooling. this also implies more energy efficiency.

Displays that offer color-character or color-graphic capabilities can be real assets. (Of course, the software system first must support the development of applications with graphic presentations.) The first concern must be the collecting and processing of real-control information. Once this information becomes reliable, its meaning and emphasis can be greatly enhanced by graphic and color presentation. Graphic and color capability should exist in the future phases of display-terminal use. A graphic is worth 10,000 numbers. One of the most effective uses of real-control information is for management by exception (looking for deviations from plan). Graphic representations are much more effective for visually denoting patterns and vectors of deviations or trends than rows of numbers. Color provides additional clarity.

Word-processing capabilities are also important services to consider relative to terminal characteristics. The paper mills of the offices also need to be computerized. Word processing covers a whole array of functions that allows textual and documentary-information processing to be computerized. This function includes techniques such as paragraph blocking; pagination; table, figure, and paragraph indexing; table of contents generation; spelling checkers; and even electronic-mailing capabilities.

These capabilities can greatly improve office productivities but are especially effective when they can be fed by the central-system data base, and the documentary data in such systems can be fed into the central system. Stand-alone mini-word-processing systems are not ideal solutions. Ideally, the capabilities should be a functional part of the main system that processes the real-control information of the operation. Word-processing accessibility within the communication system of the central system makes the electronic-mail aspects especially valuable.

Auxiliary-Device Support

Assuming that the user-oriented service is being obtained from a centralized computer, the central system will provide the primary storage for data. It will also have high-speed printing and magnetic-tape systems that could be used for related data output. However, in a decentralized, display-oriented service, more is needed than just access via the terminals. The system should also allow use of auxiliary devices. These devices are usually connected through the display terminal to the communication line that makes the connection to the central system.

These auxiliary devices can be very useful and are definitely needed to complete an effective, remote-computer service. There are a number of different types of auxiliary devices offered. A variety of remote printers, diskette, and cassette units, as well as graphic plotters, are offered. The vendor's specifications will identify the features of the various devices.

The cassettes and diskettes provide selective, immediately accessible extracts of information that can be kept locally available and reloaded when needed for further processing. These provide an effective media for selective, personalized historical-data storage. Diskettes are preferable to cassettes. Access to any portion of the disk is much faster than rolling through the tape cassette.

Auxiliary print capability is essential at the remote site. Usually this capability is needed for relatively small printouts. The speed of the communication lines usually means that such printers cannot be used for large printouts consisting of many pages. Large printouts are better made at the central site on the local high-speed printers and couriered or mailed to the remote site. Selective prints of small sets of current control information are very valuable and need to be made as required at the local site. A good, fast remote-print device should be purchased. Quick printing allows effective use of the terminals as well as the associated communication line. The bidirectional remote auxiliary printers are usually best; print quality is an important consideration in choosing these devices. Another desirable feature is to be able to use the display terminal while the connected printer is printing.

Tools for System Coordination

The job role and philosophies related to effective coordination of a Free Enterprise Computing service have already been discussed in this book. To be effective, a coordinator needs certain tools and controls that give the visibilities of activity and disciplines that can be administered to ensure a powerful, system-safe service. These tools must be considered essential in choosing the best system for a particular operation. In fact, looking for these tools in the system-selection process will cause an automatic, justified elimination of many of the current "user-friendly" system offering that do not have them.

Another name for "free enterprise" conducted in a state where there are no law, police, or courts of justice is "anarchy". *Anarchy* would also describe the result of a user-oriented system that lacked the controls to provide adequate security, monitoring facilities, and the means to assure performance according to application plan.

The coordination tools should be evaluated early in the consideration of any system. The lack of these controls indicates an immature system concept. A vendor of a system that lacks these essential controls has sensed the demand for user-oriented systems, but this vendor lacks the extensive, in-depth experience to realize that offering the cosmetics of a user-oriented service without the support tools to coordinate and effectively control such a service is a formula for disaster.

To be effective, coordination exercises control of a Free Enterprise Computing service in four major areas; namely, the community, data-base planning, transactional use, and communication-systems use. Users must be individually registered and capable of being specifically, functionally limited. Data base is managed by controlling a planned application turn-on and by having the ability to monitor base growth and maintenance. Data-base security controls must also be established with the base. Transactional use is controlled by having the ability to examine activity of the moment as well as records of entire days of use. The primary goal of these controls is to assure plan-to-actual application control. The application is planned relative to its data-base size and impact on resources, and then actual use is monitored in real-time to assure performance to plan. The coordinator must also be responsible for security administration in all four areas.

To control the users of a Free Enterprise Computing service, it is essential that the chosen system provides the ability to register the users as individuals and to specifically turn on or off the functional capabilities for each of them. This is required to ensure system safety.

A user may begin as a procedural user of a system by being allowed only to execute prepared report-generation sequences. If the user develops general-purpose skills such as the ability to use search or sort functions or some of the computational functions, then these are turned on for the user to execute.

If the user masters the basic, general-purpose, functional skills and is attracted to report-generator designing, this ability is turned on for use. Coordination functional capabilities are set for use only by coordinators. System-support functions such as recovery or history production are reserved to system-support personnel. Clearly, all functional capabilities are not suitable for all users. Discrimination based on skill level and operational need is an imperative for overall system safety.

Data-base control begins with a data plan. Each application, as it is implemented, is planned to rise to a certain level of real-time data content and then cycle at that level with an influx of new information. As every viable system must do, a flow in and out must be part of the design to avoid an unhealthy bloat. It is the essence of real-control information that it must consist of information concerning that which is about to enter the operation, that which is in the operation, and that which has just left the operation. If these criteria are not met, what the computer is handling is data, not information. As historical data develops in the on-line base, it must be separated from the real-time information on which Free Enterprise Computing is based.

The key to data-base control then is an ability to compare planned to actual data-base condition and to denote exceptions. An exception to plan may involve a base that is not being promptly cleaned of historical data as it develops. Or it may be a base that becomes stagnant due to a failure of the plan. Either case represents a deviation from plan and must be dealt with by coordination.

For data-base control, the chosen system should have the tools to monitor, summarize, and reflect actual data-base conditions. Characteristics of this reflection that are essential to control are; an indication of data-set sizes, the date of the last update, and the frequency of updates. Automated tools to monitor and control the Free Enterprise Computer data base are essential for coordination to ensure that the valuable resource is effectively used according to plan.

In addition to providing a means to eliminate inactive data from the system, tools should be provided to automate the deletion process. Examples of such undesirable data would be duplicate sets of data or reports that are no longer updated and really constitute deadwood in the system. Manual clean-up methods used by coordination will not be adequate to this task once the service becomes sizeable; therefore, it is imperative that automated tools be available to identify the existence of this obsolete data and to alert the user-community so they can be involved in the clean-up process (getting back to plan).

The administration of overall security is a coordinator responsibility. Security techniques must be available to limit data accessibility to the proper users. Password accessibility to data is a common technique. However, in the case of very sensitive data, such as personnel records, pay, or budgets, it must be possible to limit access to specific stations and users, and the use of hieroglyphic password algorithms are essential. Security clearance should distinguish between retrieval-only access and access with update and data change capability. Password to update protection must be available at the report or data-set level.

The basis of control of transactional use of the system by the user-community is a satisfactory set of transactional records. This is a record of each functional process executed by the users. Minimum statistics needed are:

Sign-on name of the user

Station number of the display or device used

Time of the execution

Response time of the execution

Indications of which data was processed

An accounting key for service charges

Measurements of amount of data processed

Indications of what portions of the system resource were used

The chosen system must have the ability to continually accumulate such transactional statistical records in a log file as the system is used.

One log file would be accumulated for each day of use. The system must provide the ability to keep multiple sets of daily logs on-line for access to the current log as well as to historical logs for coordination analysis. Real-time functions must be provided to produce summaries as well as detailed information about transaction use. These functions should be capable of selecting from the log specifically or in combination based on:

Name of user executing

Station used

Time slot (beginning and end)

Function used

Function time active

Data accessed

Current or prior day's log

This transaction-log data provides the basis of transactional-use monitoring. Its use is primarily based on exception analysis (looking for abnormal or abusive use). The real-time, log-analysis functions allow quick access to any portion of the log based on parameters selected to allow specific analysis of particular characteristics of use.

It is also advantageous if coordination tools are provided to allow sorted-summary-batch analysis of the entire day's log to determine characteristics such as:

How individual users used the system

How individual displays were used

How individual functions were used

How much related sets of data were used

Batch analysis of the log file can also provide graphic profiles over time that show peaks and valleys of the system resource throughout the operating day. These profiles are useful to determine unusual peaks that can be specifically analyzed with the real-time log-analysis functions. They can also be an aid to provide effective scheduling of larger report generators into low-use time periods.

The ability to obtain visibility of current, instantaneous use is also an important control capability for effective coordination. This is needed when a particularly unusual loading condition is being noted on the system or monitoring of a current process is desired. When it is felt that the system is laboring or perhaps delays are being encountered on parts of the system, it is extremely valuable for a coordinator to obtain a snap of information showing functional concurrency of the moment. This should give the kind of information that will enable the coordinator to detect abusers and identify the station they are operating on and the process they are using. It should also provide indications of levels of system resource in use.

As the number of on-line displays build on the system-communication network, network management becomes a major concern of an effective coordination function. This is especially a problem when the terminals are not only on local communication lines within the operation but even more so when the service is being delivered through the general telephone systems to remote locations.

To have effective communication-system control, the system should provide real-time monitoring that provides:

Current status of individual stations

Time of last traffic

Error rates on lines and terminals

Types of errors encountered

Transfer loads on communication lines

In a small system, all this coordination control and visibility may not seem necessary. But, again, the potential of a real-time, Free Enterprise Computing service should not be underestimated. If a system is selected that does not have these control capabilities, great difficulty will be encountered later on when demand causes the service to grow. It is very difficult to build these control capabilities into the system later on. Of course, a system switch should also be avoided if at all possible. So the correct approach is to choose a mature system with all these capabilities in place and useable as the service is built and grows.

16 Putting Free Enterprise Computing into Your Operation

Making a decision to implement Free Enterprise Computing in your operation or company will be one of the most important decisions that can be made. Its effects will not only be quickly felt but will have enormous long-range benefits and implications. The dissemination and use of computer power throughout all areas of your operation, from the most clerical to the most executive, allows a powerful catalytic energy to permeate the operation.

It manifests itself as measurable, immediate productivity improvement as the existing multitudes of manually controlled paper operations bring computer power into use. These are not small but very large increments of productivity improvement at the most labor- and material-intensive levels. And because so many operations can be quickly affected, great productivity gains are achieved throughout the operation. As these applications become polished and reliable, a sense of accuracy and confident controllability permeates the organization.

From the bases of departmental, computerized, real-control information, the flow of status reporting to upper management becomes timely, more accurately reflective of reality, and more dependable. As the end-users develop their report-processing skills and patterns of repetitive functional use are identified, the development of report generators is implemented where appropriate to improve computer efficiencies.

As these cells of computerized control information form, and the paths of information flow evolve, a vibrant system of control information communication establishes itself. With this comes productivity and efficiency improvement that becomes apparent throughout all operations. Lead times are reduced, processing times are shortened because the delays in manual information manipulation to accomplish decision making have been eliminated. Process expediting is no longer manual. Priority decisions are made accurately in seconds and communicated to all concerned from a common reference. In-process inventories shrink because decision-making queues are reduced. Real-time computerized exception reporting is a key to all this control.

Important productivity gains are achieved wherever this new-found computing power is applied. But the most important aspect of all this accomplishment is the fact that the power of the computer has been placed directly in the hands of the end-users. This accomplishes enormous efficiencies in application design and implementation because of the elimination of the data-processing middlemen in the design process. But what is even more important for the long term is the fact that all this computer power can be made to conform to the requirements of growth and change, the only certain elements in most operations. The computer power is adapted to new policies, directions, and needs by the people in charge as required. Through Free Enterprise Computing, the computer has been made into a utilitarian tool and placed in the hands of the results-oriented operations people, the supervisors, managers, directors, and executives who are responsible for real accomplishment. The bottleneck of the system that requires a data-processing professional has been bypassed.

The managers who lead the move to this new form of information management become notable for their accomplishment. Just as concepts of free enterprise and decentralization have had powerful motivational effects in societal and corporate environments, a similar effect is obtained from the introduction of Free Enterprise Computer power into these operational environments. The ability to get at and mold and control computer power is exciting and even addictive. The results achieved are often dramatic. A strong sense of accomplishment and pride of ownership are notable characteristics in application implementation by these end-users. They become Free Enterprise Computing's best advocates.

17 Rights to Support Free Enterprise Computing

It should be clear that the most effective implementation of Free Enterprise Computing occurs in an information-processing environment that fosters natural processes of decentralization, innovation, and learning processes unrestrained by arbitrary resource limitations, in other words, granting certain rights, powers, and protections to the user-community. These are enumerated in the following "Free Enterprise Computer User's Bill of Rights."

Free Enterprise Computer User's Bill of Rights

1. *Data processing shall make no policy abridging the freedom of the users to operate within the planned scope of their applications.* Freedom of choice to execute necessary analytical processes within the resource planned for the application shall be a right of the users. By prescribing burdensome policies and step-by-step analytical procedures, data processing deadens the vitality of Free Enterprise Computing.
2. *The user's right to bear as much functional power, including RPG design, as is feasible with system safety and resource limitations, shall not be abridged.* Users must be given a full range of processing powers to choose from if effective Free Enterprise Computing is to be accomplished.
3. *The users shall be the primary authority regarding security measures associated with their data and accessibility thereto.* User-management must be the directors of policy relative to needed levels of security and data accessibility.
4. *The right of the users to be the ultimate authority as to the applicability of data to their operational environment shall not be violated.* Only users have the intimate knowledge of their operations environment to make the final determinations of data applicability.
5. *No user shall have to answer for a security violation or system abuse without due process of transactional evidence.* Adequate system-use records must be collected to establish data on security violations. In a Free Enterprise Computing environment, heresay and rumor cannot be accepted as evidence of abuse.

6. *Users have the right to see all evidence of security or system abuse presented against them.* A user charged with data or security abuses has a right to see the recorded evidence of his or her error. This not only ensures just charges but is also instructive where the abuse was accidental, as is often the case.

7. *The right of judgment and responsibility for defense of application value is reserved to the user organization.* Only the users with intimate knowledge of their operational realities can make appropriate defenses and judgments relative to application values. This also places the responsibility for justification under their responsibility.

8. *System charges in excess of resources utilized shall be neither required nor imposed by the servicing data-processing organization.* A data-processing organization that opposes the concept of user-oriented, Free Enterprise Computing will sometimes attempt to discourage the use of such services by charging punitive rates. Users should rightfully be charged for Free Enterprise Computing service only on the basis of the actual resource utilized in such computing.

9. *The right of users to decide the priorities of applications shall not be abridged, nor shall such a right be countermanded by the servicing data-processing organization.* Only real knowledge of the operational environment can form a sound basis for priority setting relative to the applications of Free Enterprise Computing. The involvement of the data-processing department must be strictly as a consultant and service source.

10. *The primary functions of system coordination shall be to ensure system safety and to maximize the effectiveness of planned resource utilization. All other rights of service determination are reserved to the users.* The coordinator's prime concern must be that of the total system and service delivered. Without the system, no service is possible, so system safety is a primary concern in all coordination processes. Promotion of efficiency is a secondary concern recognizing that, widely promoted, efficiency benefits the entire service. She or he must also be cognizant of application plans and must ensure operations within the resources allocated to the plans. Security concerns are also fundamental. All other aspects of Free Enterprise Computing must be reserved to the control of the users to ensure effective utilization.

18 The MAPPER System: Proof of Free Enterprise Computing Concepts

The concepts of Free Enterprise Computing, as defined in this book, are proven in extensive real-life experience. Sperry Univac began developing the concepts of report processing in 1968. It has been implemented throughout the corporation in numerous systems. These systems provide real-time report-processing services to networks of display terminals ranging from a few hundred to over one thousand each. Thousands of users have designed and implemented thousands of reporting applications that are processed with millions of transactions per day. Hundreds of millions of lines of report data are processed daily to produce real-control information in Sperry Univac's many plants.

Sperry Univac markets the MAPPER 1100 Report Processing System as a software product. Many customer sites are in existence with MAPPER systems in use. Some of these are larger services than those operating in Sperry Univac. The following section describes some of the characteristics of Sperry Univac's MAPPER Report Processing System and some examples of system use.

Sperry Univac MAPPER 1100 CRT Report-Processing System

MAPPER: A Software Product

The MAPPER (Maintaining, Preparing, and Producing Executive Reports) Report Processing System is a Sperry Univac proprietary software product. It was developed by Evaluation Programming in Sperry Univac, Roseville Operations. The primary inventors of the concepts of report processing are: William R. Gray, Charles A. Hanson, Lynn E. Mielke, and Louis Schlueter. The innovative recommendations of the report-processing system user-community have also been a rich source of valuable enhancements.

The CRT report-processing concept has been in development and use since 1968. It has been successfully installed in numerous high-volume 1100 installations both within Sperry Univac and at customer sites. Some of these installations provide CRT report-processing services to thousands of users with hundreds of terminals on-line. The largest of these sites handles over a million transactions per day where over 100 million lines of report data are processed (displayed, searched, sorted, printed, and so on).

The Univac 1100 CRT Report Processing/Generating System (MAPPER 1100) is a general-purpose, real-time report-processing system that uses UNISCOPE display terminals and auxiliary print-storage devices. MAPPER uses a "report-structured" data base that is specifically designed to support high-volume, random-access, real-time CRT report processing. Real-time updating is supported with complete data-base management, recovery, and historical-access capabilities. The system is capable of report entry, storage, retrieval, real-time update/change, display, and hard-copy output. Report processing can be done with over eighty functions such as search, sort, matching, and calculation. Functions for date analysis, character-string location and change and Fortran-like equation solving are also available. A start and retrieve interface to the 1100 batch environment can be used as well as a station-to-station message-delivery service. Where repetitive relationships of functional use exist in MAPPER, a RUN function can be designed and used. This simple, quickly implemented, user-oriented language provides a powerful report-generating capability and also a means of automating MAPPER data-base updating. Complete formating flexibility is possible. The selected functional sequence of a given RUN may be interspersed with logical decisions made on results produced or on memory (variables) accumulated. The decisions may affect functional jumping, branching based on data content. The RUN may be designed to be used in a tutorial mode allowing sequential interruption for display and interactive parameter entry. The RUN design process itself is interactive with immediate diagnostic responses provided.

A MAPPER to MAPPER remote RUN capability makes intersystem data linking possible.

Form Generation: Applications
Programming Eliminated

A unique feature of MAPPER 1100 is a form-generation capability that allows implementation of data bases and related report processing and generating services without applications programming. To establish a new reporting application in MAPPER, the user defines the report headers or form as he or she would like to see it on the display in a free-form experimental report. The MAPPER coordinator then executes a function called Form Generation against this header (form) definition. This function locks onto this form definition and automatically establishes:

Form protection: headers and tab field dividers

Edit control for each character position

Data-base management:
  Automatic schema definition
  Immediate support of real-time updating
  Recovery and history back-up

Masks for function control

Immediate processing with the functions of MAPPER (the functions automatically adjust to data format during execution)

This form-generation process, the turn-on of an easily updated, real-time application, is done in minutes.

By eliminating the role of the applications programmer through form generation, the user can conveniently begin and modify reporting formats as his or her experience grows. He or she can do this without the frequent communication problems and costs of applications programming. The programming cost savings provided by this approach are obviously significant. But, of even greater importance, is the flexibility and user convenience of this environment. An exceptional degree of user satisfaction and pride in their reporting is attained. This is because they themselves design their reports. The reports are conveniently and quickly implemented exactly as they were intended. The report performs the real-time reporting task as the user feels it should be done considering his or her unique requirements, work environment, and experience. The user can conveniently change to better formats as experience and ingenuity allows or as his or her management directs.

MAPPER and the 1100 Environment

MAPPER 1100 operates as a real-time application within the 1100 operating-system environment. Extensive use of other real-time, demand, and batch systems can be made in the same system with MAPPER. A heavy mix is possible with proper scheduling and file assignment.

Batch-Data Interfaces to MAPPER

Batch runs may be started (batch start) from MAPPER to the 1100 operating system with run-stream-include statements. Thus data collected in MAPPER can be passed into batch runs, or simple batch-program starts can be made.

Batch data can be retrieved into MAPPER 1100 reports from 1100 SDF (print) files in real-time. Report processing then is used to make such records more valuable.

Manually Executable Report Processing Functions

□ Display Report
□ Add Report
□ Delete Report
□ Duplicate Report
□ Add Line
□ Delete Line
□ Duplicate Line
□ Search Report (See Example)
□ Search Update Report
□ Find (positional search)
□ Sort Report
□ Print Reports
□ Index Reports
□ Search List
□ Totalize (data compute)
□ Replace Report
□ Punch (card output)
□ Arithmetic (equation solver)
□ Match Reports
□ Match Update Reports
□ Reformat Reports
□ Remote Auxiliary Device Output (print, cassette, diskette)
□ Historical Data/Batch File Access
□ Batch Start
□ Batch File Retrieve
□ Append Report
□ Message Switching (station to station)
□ Locate (character string)
□ Change (character string)
□ Date Analyzer
□ Demand Processing (RSI)
□ Remote System Run (via data link)

Report Processing Functions Usable in Run Functions

□ Display
□ Arithmetic (equation solver)
□ Search (field or fields)
□ Search Update (reports)
□ Search List
□ Search List Update
□ Read Line
□ Write Line
□ Read Continuous
□ Index
□ Match (reports)
□ Match Update
□ Add To (append)
□ Add On (append)
□ Date (analyzer)
□ Locate (character string)
□ Message Switching
□ If (qualification)
□ CHG (variable change)
□ GO TO (branching)
□ Rename (result save)
□ OUT (to display)
□ Wait (stall)
□ Tape Cassette
□ Totalize (data compute)
□ Sort
□ Replace Report
□ Delete Report
□ Print (high speed)
□ Batch Start
□ Find (positional search)
□ Auxiliary print
□ Reform (form change)
□ Add Report
□ Duplicate Report
□ RUN (start another Run function)
□ Remote Run (start a Run in a remote MAPPER via data link)
□ Patch Port (MAPPER as remote processor)
□ Variable (memory cells)
□ LOG (run logging)
□ SUB (subtotaling function)
□ Line Add, Delete, Duplicate

Figure 18-1. Report-Processing Functions

**A key to the "User Friendly" simplicity
of the MAPPER Language is the fact that:**

**The function parameters are submitted
in the context of the user's own data**

Examples of Search Input Parameters

Search Logic	```*ST.STATUS.BY. PRODUCT .SERIAL.PRODUC.ORDER.CUST.PRODUC.``` ```*CD. DATE .IN. TYPE .NUMBER. COST .NUMBR.CODE. PLAN .```
-----------------------------	```*==.======.==.=========.======.======.=====.====.======.``` ```** ****** ** ********* ****** ****** ***** **** ******```
Single Identifier	SH
Multiple Identifier	SC SH
and Condition (Masked)	SH BLACKBOX/
Search in Range	 R 500000 700000

Examples of Sort Input Parameters

Sort Logic	```*ST.STATUS.BY. PRODUCT .SERIAL.PRODUC.ORDER.CUST.PRODUC.``` ```*CD. DATE .IN. TYPE .NUMBER. COST .NUMBR.CODE. PLAN .```
-----------------------------	```*==.======.==.=========.======.======.=====.====.======.``` ```** ****** ** ********* ****** ****** ***** **** ******```
Single Level Ascending	1
Single Level Descending	1D
Multiple Level	1 2
Multi-Level & Descending	1 2D

Examples of Totalizer   Input Parameters

Totalizer Logic	```* PRODUCT . SUB .PRODUC. SALES .SPACE. DEMO .``` ```* TYPE . KEY . COST .COMMISS. REQ .QUANTITY. DEMO RESULTS```						
-----------------------------	```*=========.=====.======.=======.=====.========.==============``` ```********* ***** ***** ****** ***** ******* **************```						
Vertical Sum/s			+	+	+	+	
Algebraic Sum/s			+	–	+	–	=
Extension & Sum					+	*	= +
Factor Adjustment			+10 =				
Subtotal/s	S		+		+		
Average/s			A	A	A	A	
Sub & Grand Cum	S		+			=	C

Figure 18-2. Function-Parameter Examples

MAPPER 1100 System

On—Line Data Base

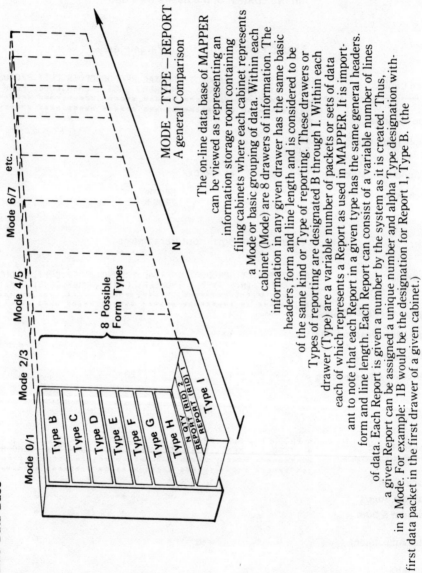

MODE — TYPE — REPORT
A general Comparison

The on-line data base of MAPPER can be viewed as representing an information storage room containing filing cabinets where each cabinet represents a Mode or basic grouping of data. Within each cabinet (Mode) are 8 drawers of information. The information in any given drawer has the same basic headers, form and line length and is considered to be of the same kind or Type of reporting. These drawers or Types of reporting are designated B through I. Within each drawer (Type) are a variable number of packets or sets of data each of which represents a Report as used in MAPPER. It is important to note that each Report in a given type has the same general headers, form and line length. Each Report can consist of a variable number of lines of data. Each Report is given a number by the system as it is created. Thus, a given Report can be assigned a unique number and alpha Type designation within a Mode. For example: 1B would be the designation for Report 1, Type B. (the first data packet in the first drawer of a given cabinet.)

Figure 18-3. On-Line, Report-Structured Data Base

Example — Report Processing
MAPPER 1100 REPORT

```
.DATE 13 DEC 79  10:49:34  RID      2    03 DEC 79  LOU1
.                CORPORATE PRODUCTION STATUS              B0022
*ST.STATUS.BY. PRODUCT .SERIAL.PRODUC.ORDER.CUST.PRODUC.PRODUC. SHIP .SHIP .SPC.
*CD. DATE .IN.  TYPE   .NUMBER. COST .NUMBR.CODE. PLAN .ACTUAL. DATE .ORDER.COD.
*==.======.==.=========.======.======.=====.====.======.======.======.=====.===.
 IP 741224 LS BLACKBOX1 436767        84389 AMCO 741223 741224
 IP 741225 LS BLACKBOX1 436768        84390 AMCO 741223 741225
 IP 741219 LS BLACKBOX2 637071        84353 INTR 741218 741219
 OR 750110 LS BLACKBOX4               94754 ARCO
 •
 •
 •
 SC 750105 LS GREENBOX8 677481        97929 INTR 750105
 IP 741225 LS GREENBOX8 750933        86381 FEDS 741225 741225
 SC 750110 LS GREENBOX8 975481        99943 AMCO 750110
 OR 740310 LS GREENBOX9               99951 AMCO
 OR 750103 LS GREENBOX9               96755 USSC
 SH 741202 LS GREENBOX9 640104        56272 FEDS 741201 741201 741202 S4528
 SH 741202 LS GREENBOX9 777321        55233 FEDS 741201 741201 741202 S8531
                   ..... END REPORT .....
```

Search Request

```
SEARCH REPORT DATA:
       RID 2
       TYPE B,
       FORMAT
```

Search Mask

```
*ST.STATUS.BY. PRODUCT .SERIAL.PRODUC.ORDER.CUST.PRODUC.PRODUC. SHIP .SHIP .SPC.
*CD. DATE .IN.  TYPE   .NUMBER. COST .NUMBR.CODE. PLAN .ACTUAL. DATE .ORDER.COD.
*==.======.==.=========.======.======.=====.====.======.======.======.=====.===.
 ** ****** ** ********* ****** ****** ***** **** ****** ****** ****** ***** ***
 SH
```

Search Result

```
.
.   10 LINES FOUND OUT OF 45 LINES
.
*** ****** ** ********* ****** ****** ***** **** ****** ****** ****** ***** ***
*SH
.
.DATE 13 DEC 79  10:49:34  RID      2    03 DEC 79  LOU1
.                CORPORATE PRODUCTION STATUS              B0022
*ST.STATUS.BY. PRODUCT .SERIAL.PRODUC.ORDER.CUST.PRODUC.PRODUC. SHIP .SHIP .SPC.
*CD. DATE .IN.  TYPE   .NUMBER. COST .NUMBR.CODE. PLAN .ACTUAL. DATE .ORDER.COD.
*==.======.==.=========.======.======.=====.====.======.======.======.=====.===.
 SH 741203 LS BLACKBOX0 746327        54237 FEDS 741201 741202 741203 S8738
 SH 741202 LS BLACKBOX6 368061        54438 FEDS 741201 741201 741202 S6937
 SH 741209 LS BLACKBOX6 777324        54232 DICO 741207 741208 741209 S8538
 SH 741203 LS BLACKBOX6 785367        52833 ARCO 741201 741202 741203 S8934
 SH 741202 LS BLACKBOX7 744627        44232 INTR 741201 741201 741202 S8531
 SH 741203 LS BLACKBOX8 945327        74272 FEDS 741201 741202 741203 S8518
 SH 741204 LS BLACKBOX9 744577        64231 AMCO 741201 741203 741204 S8531
 SH 741206 LS GREENBOX7 669624        54682 AMCO 741201 741205 741206 S8553
 SH 741202 LS GREENBOX9 640104        56272 FEDS 741201 741201 741202 S4528
 SH 741202 LS GREENBOX9 777321        55233 FEDS 741201 741201 741202 S8531
                   ..... END REPORT .....
```

Figure 18-4. Example MAPPER Report

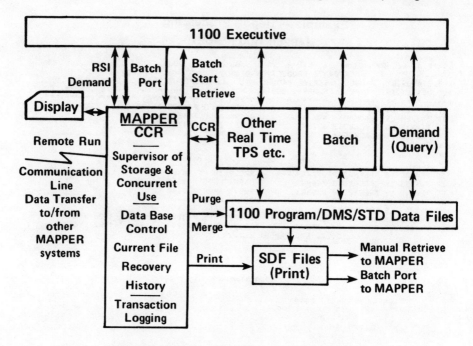

Figure 18-5. MAPPER in 1100 Environment

Batch data can be routed to the MAPPER system. A batch-port interface to MAPPER is available that causes MAPPER to appear as a
remote processor. Through this, batch SDF file data may be input to
MAPPER and a RUN started to process the data in MAPPER.

MAPPER Terminal Access to Other
Real-Time Applications

Users of terminals under MAPPER control can make calls to other real-
time applications in the 1100 environment. The MAPPER Communications
Control Routine (CCR) provides entry points through which data buffers
can be passed to and from the other applications.

MAPPER Software

MAPPER 1100 is programmed under the 1100 Operating System Assembler
and operates under the standard Sperry Univac 1100 operating system.
MAPPER operates as a real-time application in the 1100 environment. The

MAPPER software system is specifically designed to efficiently support the intense mix of activity inherent in the real-time report-processing/ generating environment and still allow demand or batch background processing under the 1100 Executive. The 1100 operating system is interfaced by MAPPER functions through a MAPPER supervisor, which controls terminal polling, function loading, and execution, memory, and file-storage allocation. Breakpoint and usage algorithms are established by which the supervisor sets priorities for all MAPPER internal activity to maximize response time, giving highest priority to low-impact transactions.

Function Program Characteristics

The report-processing or generating function programs are called to MAPPER's memory pool from rotating storage as required. They are segmented wherever possible to minimize memory requirements. The functions are reentrant to allow multiple jobs to be processed with one copy of the functions in memory. They are relocatable to allow loading into any available portion of memory and to facilitate program swapping to alleviate memory-pool binds during heavy use. All the functions are generalized and can be applied in processing on any of the types of reporting set up in the MAPPER 1100 Report Processing System, that is, they will automatically conform to the form of the report data processed during execution.

Tutorial Aids

Report-processing user procedures are on-line and accessible under the call HELP. On-line proficiency examinations as well as demonstration data bases and RUN functions are available to use for learning report-processing concepts.

Examples of field-formed reporting and RUNS that can be processed can be seen on-line in the demonstration mode. Password to access this mode can be obtained from the MAPPER system coordinators. Coordinators can also help users to obtain personal as well as terminal registration and procedures for system use.

System Coordination, Security, and Data-Base Management

An extensive array of functions, RUNs, and processes are available for the system coordinator to control and monitor systems use and performance.

Security techniques are available to provide almost any needed protection against improper data access or system abuse. Users as well as terminals are registered and controlled individually. Users may be restricted to any level of functional capability if desired. All transactional activity is logged. Real-time and batch analysers are available for transactional monitoring. Real-time and batch analyzers of communications errors and use are also provided for communications-system management. Many real-time and batch processes are available to aid the MAPPER system coordinators in system control and data-base management. The functional report-processing capabilities of MAPPER are used extensively to provide real-time control of MAPPER. Purge/merge processes are available to cycle MAPPER report data files daily. These processes develop copies of existing reports on tape for historical access. At the same time currency, quantity, and size of report data are reflected in on-line status reports. These are used by the system coordinator to monitor plan versus actual reporting performance. Fast, reliable recovery procedures are available to use in case of system, power, or hardware problems. High-volume, random-access, real-time report-processing and updating services can be supported and controlled.

MAPPER 1100 Report-Processing System:
Sperry Univac, Roseville Operations

The Sperry Univac large-scale systems design and manufacturing operations in Roseville, Minnesota, use the largest report-processing system service within the Sperry Corporation. (The world's largest MAPPER report-processing service exists at Santa Fe Railway, see chapter 20.) This service is provided from the Midwest Region Computing Center by the Major Systems Division (MSD) system (see figure 18-6). This is an 1100/82 multiprocessor system. Besides extensive conventional, structured real-time, demand and batch-processing services, it delivers a MAPPER 1100 real-time report-processing service to over 1,125 terminals. Over 100 departments are served. An average of over 350,000 report-processing transactions are performed each day in which over 85 million report data lines are processed. The on-line, real-time updated data base consists of over 6.2 million lines of report data consisting of more than 25,000 individual reports in over 1,100 different types (applications) of reporting.

With a history of report-processing implementation in the Sperry Univac, Roseville, operations since 1968, about three new reporting applications are still being turned on each week. The system utilization continues to grow at a rate of about 20 percent per year. These facts dramatically demonstrate not only an ease of real-time reporting-applications development but also give an indication of the popularity and potential of Free Enterprise Computing.

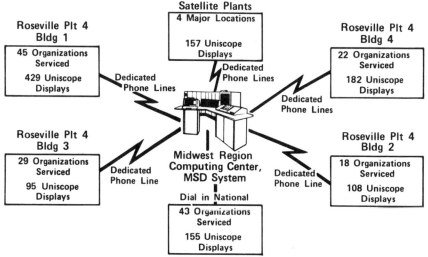

Figure 18-6. Univac MAPPER 1100 Report-Processing System

The following is a sampling of some of the over 1,100 report-processing applications in use at the Sperry Univac plants in Roseville. These applications were all designed by users in the operations. They are display-oriented, real-time applications that are randomly accessed and are totally updated on-line.

Absence records	Daily packet status
Accounting standard data	Defective-material review
A.D. software qualification	Direct labor variance
Assembly genealogy	Document-distribution control
Assembly status control	E.R.C. cable inventory
Assembly and inspection labor	Early-delivery monitor
Blanket order subcontract	Employee central file
Back-panel wire tabs	Equipment down status
Cable order log	Explosion/implosion: parts
Cable test procedures	Factory cost analysis
Card-placement status	Factory shortages
Completion analysis	Factory test lists
Component defects	Failure malfunction reporting
Customer file	FCO unit location
Cycle-inventory status	Finished-goods inventory

General orders to ship
Horizontal leveled schedule
IE assembly genealogy
Inactive/excess inventory analysis
Inbound routing
Inbound tonnage
Interfactory orders
Inventory relief and capitalization
Inventory status
LM backorder status
Maintenance stores inventory
Manpower budgeting
Material-impact analysis
Material-order status
Manufacturing EIR status
Miscellaneous required net to time
MLP quality data
New-product evaluation
Production control factors
Production leads to success (PLUS)
Production status
Productivity improvement
Purchase-order follow-up
Purchase-requisition log
Printed circuit artwork status
Printed circuit assy and board
Printed circuit scheduling
Printed circuit shortages
Quality test request for change
Quality test data
Quality laboratory report
Quality test shortages
Records retention
Returned equipment inbound

Returned equipment parts inventory
Returned equipment planning
Returned equipment product
   schedule
Returned equipment project status
Returned equipment salvage
Resource planning
Return-to-vendor status
Returned equipment assy status
RFC-EIR-FCO tracking
Roseville order status
Roseville test inventory
Semiconductor parts status
Stores crib requisitions
System requirements
Telephone equipment control
Test quality turnover
Test vehicle scheduling
Testability status
Tool catalog
Tool spares inventory
Tool and supply requisitions
Trial-balance report
Travel-balance accounting
Parts value distribution
Variance budgets
Variance exception
Visitor register
Warehouse job pull
Weekly job summary
Work requirement, plant services
Work-center scheduling
Work planning, plant operations

19 Evolution of the Report-Processing Concept

The Sperry Univac MAPPER 1100 Report Processing System is the end result of an evolutionary system design and implementation process that began in 1968. At that time, in the test department of Sperry Univac Operations in Roseville, Minnesota, a need to develop a computerized test inventory-status reporting application was defined. At that time the UNISCOPE 300 display terminals were becoming available in sizeable quantities. Therefore, it was proposed that these displays should be used to provide a medium for this inventory-status reporting and that the reporting was to be real-time in nature. These test operations accomplish the final units and systems testing of the large-scale systems of Sperry Univac. The inventory involved is large and expensive, and an extensive amount of status information is needed regarding test processes.

Had the test inventory-status application designers approached the design in a conventional way, a data base would have been designed to contain the data elements needed. Then a set of specific queries would have been designed and the logic programmed to provide specifically formulated answers to those queries. In other words, a conventional, specifically structured, real-time, transaction-oriented application would have been designed.

It was noted that the typical computer output for many computer applications was printed output of vertically field-formed lists of data with appropriate headers. In fact, it was proposed that vertically field-formed lists of test inventory data were to be provided that could be processed on-line with real-time display. These lists would have consisted of fields denoting information such as descriptions of items under test, test status codes, dates, quantities in test, and so on. Fortunately for computer users, a generalized report-processing system concept was defined instead. A specification outlining the concept of generalized CRT report processing was written in February of 1968, and this provided the basis for the Sperry Univac 418 CRT Report Processing System project from which the Sperry Univac MAPPER 1100 Report Processing System finally evolved.

The form-generation function was proposed. This function provides a means of automating form data protection and the establishment of data-base definitions and connections to data-base support facilities. It accomplishes the programming of these disciplines in a matter of minutes. The invention of this function made the report-processing system concept

generally applicable to not only the field-formed data of the initially required test inventory-status reporting application but also to any real-time
application that has a data base that can be defined in terms of vertically
field-formed data.

With form generation, an ability to automate the computerization
(programming) of vertical data form and the processing of data entered into
the form was provided. Thus real-time updating was supported, and the data
could be displayed on the screen. In these initial reports the line length was limited to 64 characters, the horizontal screen size of the UNISCOPE 300 displays. The technology to support 132-character line lengths, and horizontal
shift and formating of selected fields was not to be developed until years later.

With these capabilities, then, report data could be entered on-line,
displayed, and events could be recorded with real-time updating. Then, in
order to turn the on-line data into information, report-processing functions
were developed. Print functions for high-speed line printers and auxiliary
printers were some of the first functions developed. A search function was
also of primary necessity, and a sort ability followed soon thereafter to put
selected information into useful orders. A function called "totalizer" was
created to perform arithmetics on fields containing numbers. This allowed
vertical summing, horizontal multiplication, factoring, averaging, subtotaling, and so on.

The applicability and productivity improvements that these relatively
simple report-processing capabilities offered were truly amazing. Within a
few months many applications besides test inventory were turned on and
made operational. Test shortage expediting, labor reporting, and equipment
scheduling were applications that provided immediate useful real-time controls in test operations.

Other departments in the factory began to become aware of the potentials of this computerzied reporting capability. Demonstrations to
production-control management promptly resulted in the application work-
center status reporting to be put on-line. This became one of the most productive report-processing applications because the whole factory evolves
around work-center progress. Within a year or so, with a service involving
about twenty-five terminals in different parts of the factory, data-base efficiency problems began to develop. The random nature of real-time report
processing and the need to support real-time updating concurrently was
causing the U418 CRT-RPS system to become saturated at the I/O (in-
put/output) levels of operation.

The base structure at that time consisted of conventional files and linked
records. It used search tables of key data (inverted file structures) to locate
the records in storage. The records were variable in length. With these concepts, record scattering and table maintenance became intolerable burdens
under the influence of random, real-time updating.

A study of the characteristics of actual use at that time showed that reports usually consisted of only a few hundred data lines as a data set. Also it was found that search requests were more complex than tabled keys could support. Often the systems were processing more tabled key data than record data in search processes. It was apparent that it would be more efficient to process the record data directly in the search processes than to use table look-up methods. So the decision was made to abandon the use of search tables thereby avoiding the processing and maintenance of the search tables.

Rolling through reports was also a common requirement, and an ability to position to specific lines in the reports was also identified as key to effective report presentation on-line. So a line table was added to each report that contained pointers to the records in storage containing the specific lines of data.

With this new approach to data base, expansion of the service continued. Finished-goods and site-administration departments came on-line with their applications as well as the production, engineering, quality, receiving, and shipping departments. The applications grew to a couple hundred within the next several years. With about sixty terminals involved in the service, another data-base crisis developed. At that level of use, I/O saturation again occurred, and the designers had to take another look at the processing realities of this random-access, report-processing service with extensive real-time updating supported. From this analysis, several additional changes in data-base concepts were implemented that led to the current data-base concept used by the MAPPER system called the "report-structured data base."

It was determined that I/O saturation was primarily being caused by two factors: line table maintenance during updating and record scattering in storage due to random updating. The studies showed that the average report consisted of 500 lines or less of data. This was a natural sizing characterstic for this type of report-processing service. Also it was noted that, because most of the report data consisted of lines containing a consistent number of fields of data, most lines for a given application were the same length and consumed the same amount of space in storage. Based on these facts pertinent to the unique nature of this service, the report was organized in a new data concept as a set of contiguous relative data in storage. This report data set made it possible to eliminate record linkage and thereby record scattering. It also made it possible to eliminate the line tables and thereby the associated line table maintenance.

These concepts, when implemented, completed the evolution to the report-structured data-base concepts that constitute modern data-base concepts. They are capable of supporting very large volumes of random-access reporting simultaneously entered from many terminals as well as high volumes of real-time updating. This report-structured data-base concept is ideal to support the random processing and updating associated with the computerization of real-control information. Not only is this data-base concept capable of supporting high volumes of real-control information processing, it is also a data-base concept that is simple enough for end-users to organize and manage. It is also possible to organize the base with indexing and algorythmic structures for larger quantities of data.

The report-structured data base has been called an *electronic-file-cabinet* concept. As simply as users can organize packets of data within file cabinets, so can they practically organize reports, the equivalent of packets, within the types of reporting (equivalent to the drawers in the file cabinet). A packet or packets in a file cabinet can contain index data that will identify the packets containing specific data items in a filing system containing large amounts of information. The reports in the report-structured data base can be similarly indexed and organized. Calculated, algorythmic access methods are also possible.

The characteristics of the report data set and its associated data structure permeated not only the design of report processing and updating functions, it also forced new recovery and history-backup techniques to be designed. User-transparent recovery-reduction and history-capturing techniques were evolved along with fast, reliable recovery methods to deal with the possible conditions of system failure.

While the evolution of the data-base concept is briefly summarized here, it was by no means accomplished without considerable trial, error, occasional traumatic data loss, and considerable downtime while data-base management bugs were worked out. At times great demands were put on the patience of the factory user-community as reliability and speed were carefully designed into the MAPPER system. Unfortunately, a system such as the MAPPER system can be debugged only in real use with high volumes of processing. A simulated test environment cannot be created for such a system. With real-time report processing becoming an indispensable, utilitarian service in the factory operations, when systems outages occurred, immediate and emotional user pressure was a powerful catalyst in the debug environment.

With the definition of the report-structured data base, another major change was affected in the system. Prior to this time, the central computer for the service was the Sperry Univac 418 computer system. About this time, the company was terminating production of this type of computer. The value of the report-processing concept had been clearly proven by the many applications in production use in many of the key departments of the operation. So a decision was made to not only adopt a report data-base structure but also to switch the concept to the Sperry Univac 1100 Systems, the mainline products of the corporation. At that time it was also named MAPPER, an acronym that stands for maintaining, preparing, and producing executive reports.

About this time in the evolution of report-processing concepts, the ability to exchange data with other systems became an added functional capability. To start with, this interface was primarily used as a means of exchanging test data between the report-processing system and other test systems. Eventually it grew into a service for all kinds of data interchange.

As the popularity of report-processing concepts expanded in the factory, the position and role of a system coordinator became a necessity. The position was established, and the coordinator became the focal point to which the users came for education, advice, assistance, and guidance in application design and implementation. The coordinator also acted as a catalyst in stimulating uses in areas with the greatest potential for benefits.

The role of system coordinator developed along with concepts of report processing over the years. Not only were the duties and principles of this new profession defined as needs and perceptions of the real nature of coordination became clear, the special tools needed for this task were also created, honed, and polished to allow an effective performance of these coordination tasks.

Transactional logging of the characteristics of use of the system was introduced and made effective with selective, real-time transaction-analysis functions. Batch processors were also developed that summarized all transactions in many ways to give perspectives on the use of the system. Database control also was addressed when an accumulation of inactive reporting became noticeable. Means for automatic base analysis and deadwood reporting elimination were developed and put into effect. Tools to determine instantaneous-use and peaking-use patterns were also created to give powerful elements of control to the system coordinators. Unique and powerful security techniques were devised to ensure system and data safety.

It is accurate to say that in the earlier years, coordination functioned largely on an intuitive basis. Determination of what went on in the system was primarily on the basis of a lot of detective-like work using questionable feedback from the user-community. Today, due to the extensive repertoire of tools and methods available in the MAPPER Report Processing System, a MAPPER coordinator is better characterized as capable of being omniscient and omnipotent in the determination of actual system use.

Unfortunately this power, when used by a coordination function that is less than ideally sensitive to the potentials of a Free Enterprise approach to use of the system, can stifle the innovation and potential productivity that could be obtained from a fuller involvement of the user-community. This is the unfortunate situation at some MAPPER system sites that have been installed over the years.

Initially most of the user education was accomplished by demonstrations conducted on a one-to-one basis with key people in the departments or in small groups by the coordinator. Then a demonstration sequence display manual was set up. This was a "cookbook" for using report-processing services. It was based on an on-line demonstration data base. By following the "cookbook" exercises on a display terminal, a user could learn the more popular functions on his or her own. This do-it-yourself education became an important multiplier in the evolution and expansion of the report-processing services. It also provided the basis for the development of detailed user reference manuals, classes, on-line tuitional aids, and video training aids.

With the transition of the report-processing concept to the Sperry Univac 1100, the service continued to expand. It moved into the receiving, purchasing, and plant engineering departments. Also, many users were seen to be repetitively using the functions of report processing in sequence to accomplish various data analysis. This precipitated the development of an ability to define function-control statements in reports for repetitive report generation by executing the specified list. In the initial phases, the process of creating the functional lists was called Report Build Generation (RBG). The execution of the sequence was called Report Generation (RPG). These concepts and techniques were refined and improved and ultimately evolved into the present RUN function language available in the MAPPER system.

The bright, innovative members of the user-community who had had extensive experience in using the functions to solve problems and accomplish report processing manually had incidentally learned the power of the instructions for the RUN function language by using them on their own self-designed data bases. Given their operational knowledge of the problems to be solved and their report-processing computer-use experience, many found the design of RUN function report generators to be a feasible and proper next skill to be developed and used in their daily pursuit of factory management. Hundreds of RUN designers were developed in the factory user-community. These were assemblers, dispatchers, secretaries, supervisors, managers, and directors. They designed and implemented thousands of report generators (RUNs) in all departments of the factory. The net result was a computerization of factory information that would have been clearly unattainable through conventional data-processing services.

The power in user-computerized real-time report processing was most notable in the production-control department of the factory. They were introduced to report processing in about 1970. At that time only manual functional report processing was possible. Direct real-time report updating and processing was done in applications such as work-center status reporting, schedule maintenance, dispatching, and shortage expediting. Extensive benefits were quickly realized over the previously used manual, paper-reporting methods.

The management of production control realized that the benefits of the use of report processing were extremely important to the control of their operation. In fact, it soon became a basic requirement that all supervisory and managerial members of the production-control department had to become skilled in report-processing capabilities.

This insistence on the development of report-processing skills had a profound effect on this department. They established a complete computerized control over every facet of their operation. Not only was complete transactional and statistical computer control established over every job and inventory item, but an evolution to an ability to do complex resource-impact projection ("what if" studies) was accomplished. Proposed schedule changes are now thoroughly analyzed in terms of impact on resources, facilities, and manpower before they are committed to. Extensive "what if" considerations are examined with complex report generations. The production-control department is now developing the use of color-graphic trend projection to enhance exception-reporting techniques. Seeing this advanced state of computer control makes it difficult for some to believe that the applications were all designed by the production-control personnel themselves.

The test department also elevated the use of MAPPER real-time report processing to high levels of sophistication. This department had the need to establish real-time test inventory-status reporting that precipitated the initial invention of the concept of CRT report processing. They implemented numerous manual report-processing applications to control their inventories, shortage expediting, and test status reporting. These evolved into sophisticated report-generator-driven applications that provide complete visibility and control of test operations.

The test department also established a network of 1100 test computers that were used to exercise the equipment under test. The necessary diagnostic-test routines are distributed throughout this network, and resultant test data is collected for centralized error-and-trend analysis. Key to the effectiveness of this test network is the use of MAPPER reporting systems operating in all the network computers to provide a common means of organizing test diagnostic routines and a test-result data-collection media. Color graphics are also now being employed in reporting test-data analysis. This is especially effective in denoting data trend-and-exception analysis.

The user-community was clearly the driving, forming force in the shaping of the repertoire of report-processing capabilities and options. The evaluation programming department, which has the basic responsibility to develop the report-processing system, always stressed a sensitivity to user desires. They solicited and responded to enhancement recommendations from the user-community. New capabilities were designed into the system if they had value and were generally useful in all reporting applications. Capabilities unique to specific application were generally rejected. Major new levels of report-processing capabilities were continually added to the system and are still being added. These are tested and stabilized on an 1100/82 development system with over 600 display terminals active. The changes are then released to the main production system in Roseville, an 1100/82 with 1,500 registered terminals. After stabilization in these large user environments, the new levels are released to qualification sites outside of Sperry Univac. After qualification at these sites, the new capabilities become available to the general customer community. By virtue of having undergone testing and stabilization in these large user environments, the MAPPER 1100 Report Processing System software exhibits unusual reliability in use. This reliability is reinforced greatly by the fact that the software of the prior release levels have been in use in many systems for many years.

The MAPPER 1100 Report Processing System was first marketed in 1976 to the Santa Fe Railway Company and shortly after that to GTE Automatic Electric, Inc. Soon after that, Goeken Systems, Inc., and Sargent Lundy Corporation also acquired MAPPER capabilities. In 1979 Sperry Univac announced the general availability of the MAPPER System as a software product. In 1981 it was introduced in Sperry Univac International Division marketing, and the system is now being translated for use in many languages.

The MAPPER system was also adopted as a standard service in the data-processing centers throughout the Sperry Corporation. It operates in conjunction with the structured conventional systems in the computer utilities, thus providing the corporation with powerful computerized administrative reporting.

The evolution of the report-processing system concepts are not complete. The user's wish list is longer today than it has ever been. It is remarkable that this is true after a continuous development of capabilities since 1968. Truly, when users finally are allowed to directly influence computer development and use, a veritable flood of applicability ensues.

20 Santa Fe Railway's OX Project: The World's Largest User-Developed Computer System

Stephen M. Anderson with
Jim C. Shepard,
K.K. Langfeld, and
W.D.Thomson

The first commercial use of Sperry Univac's MAPPER was on the Santa Fe Railway in 1976. Since Santa Fe was the first and by far the largest of the MAPPER implementations, a spirit of cooperation developed that greatly accelerated the growth of MAPPER as an ultra-high-level language. Santa Fe got a great deal from this exchange as well. According to James Martin, an internationally recognized expert and consultant on data processing, Santa Fe's OX (Operations Expeditor) project (the corporate name for the applications that used MAPPER) is the world's largest user-developed computer system and a prime example of the path data processing will have to take worldwide by the 1990s.

To understand the process that brought MAPPER to Santa Fe and the OX project to successful completion, Santa Fe itself must be understood. Santa Fe Railway is a wholly owned subsidiary of Santa Fe between Chicago and the South Pacific coast at Los Angeles and San Francisco, with other major lines down to the Gulf of Mexico through the heart of Texas. The most important commodities shipped are grains, minerals (mainly coal, potash, and sulfur), and merchandise. The railway has long been considered one of the premier railroads in the United States in terms of size, progressiveness, and dedication to high-quality service for time-sensitive freight. Timeliness proved to be the critical factor in the selection and success of MAPPER, as will be seen later.

The railway operates over 12,000 route miles of track with almost 2,000 locomotives, 66,500 cars, and 34,000 employees. With 1980 revenues of more than $2 billion (plus $158,489,000 in after-tax income), Santa Fe is a very large (and profitable) company. More than one-fourth of the revenue was from merchandise freight transportation, mostly in the form of Trailer-On-Flat-Car, or TOFC, operations. Sometimes called *piggyback* for

Stephen M. Anderson is Plus OX Coordinator; Jim C. Shepard is director, client relations, for the Information Systems Department; K.K. Langfeld is manager for operating systems; and W.D. Thomson, deceased, was assistant director, operating systems. This chapter is reprinted with the permission of the Santa Fe Railway Company.

obvious reasons, the loading of highway truck trailers on railroad flatcars can save fuel costs over highway cartage while giving railroads a way to compete for high-value traffic even if the shipper or receiver is not on a railroad spur track. But to make use of this advantage, the railroad has to provide consistently excellent service, or the traffic will revert to highway transport.

Piggyback service generates paper blizzards of forms, reports, and tracers. Records must be kept of every trailer entering or leaving the railroad piggyback yard and of where the trailers are put on or taken off the railroad cars. This process, better known as *ramping* or *deramping*, also requires records. When a trailer is deramped and temporarily stored until the owner comes to get it, its location needs to be recorded. The exact time and condition of each trailer must be recorded each time it passes between the street and the piggyback yard through a gate named for Santa Fe's Navajo indian-boy advertising trademark, Checkpoint Chico. After this long and involved process, a waybill, or combination shipping paper/invoice, must be prepared to travel with the trailer on the car.

Among other records required, the trailer owner must be charged a storage and usage fee if the trailer is stored too long on the railroad's property. This "detention" charge, if not assessed properly, can result in huge fines from the Interstate Commerce Commission. In 1973, when at last the growth of piggyback service had completely buried Corwith (the Santa Fe's Chicago rail/piggyback yard) in paperwork, and the detention was far behind and getting worse, the ICC levied a sizeable fine against Santa Fe. Worse yet, they made it completely clear that more and bigger fines would be assessed if the situation were not remedied soon.

A similar impasse had occurred in piggyback billing at Corwith. The process of matching bills of lading to the movement waybill after the shipment was enroute had become impossible. A clerk might receive a bill of lading that matched with a movement bill held by the clerk at the next desk. But the indexing and locating process had become so overwhelming that they would never make the proper connection.

Worse yet, the number of trailers to be moved from Chicago to Los Angeles peaked in the evenings, especially on Thursday and Friday. Since the Santa Fe was selling super service, there was often as little as an hour between trailer arrival at Checkpoint Chico to train departure. It was almost physically impossible to type a hundred bills per train in that time, especially when a piggyback train might leave every fifty minutes on Thursday or Friday evening. And finally, each waybill had to be manually put in extract format and transmitted by paper-tape input through a teletype so that the central computer system at Topeka, Kansas, could know that the shipment was enroute. Unfortunately, Friday's waybill extracts usually made it into Topeka on Sunday afternoon or later because of the backlog problem, which was just hours before a shipment to Los Angeles or San Francisco would arrive.

It was clear to management that something had to be done. Corwith is the largest piggyback facility on earth. In terms of intermodal facilities (places where different forms of transportation interchanged shipments such as a piggyback or truck container onto a steamship at ocean ports), Corwith is not all that much smaller than places like the container terminals at San Francisco or Rotterdam. Los Angeles was handling two-thirds of the amount at Corwith, and San Francisco and Houston about one-third. It was obviously just a matter of time until the 20 percent per year growth in intermodal traffic on Santa Fe created numerous copies of the mess at Corwith.

The clerical problems were far beyond solution by manual methods. If clerks sitting side by side could not match up huge stacks of paper, hiring more clerks who would have to sit on opposite sides of a large office might actually have a negative effect on the amount of paperwork completed. This overload had been foreseen as early as 1972, and a committee was formed, including an accountant, Jimmie C. Shepard, and two local Corwith supervisors, Jim Lind and Jim Bennecke. The "Corwith Committee" studied every data element required to handle the clerical requirements and came up with punchcard layouts to work with the IBM 360/20 computer then in use. These cards were carefully laid out so that they could transmit teletype records as well. The committee's plan was to ultimately have these layouts put on a computer and bypass the card functions completely.

The Corwith plan was finished in 1974, but the timing was bad as far as Corwith's needs were concerned. Shortly before, Santa Fe's directors had approved construction of an ultramodern railroad "hump," or gravity yard, at the junction of the Los Angeles and San Francisco lines at Barstow, California. Part of the Barstow specification was that it be computerized wherever possible, and the amount of money to be spent dictated that Santa Fe's information-systems department, or ISD, dedicate everyone available to getting Barstow ready for operation in early 1976. While ISD was using the Corwith committee's report as a system specification, the fact that Barstow had almost no billing and no originating or terminating piggyback traffic meant that all effort was concentrated on writing programs to move railcars through quickly.

It was planned from the start that the final Barstow system would be installed at Corwith and expanded to cover billing and piggyback, but this could not occur before 1977 if Barstow was to go into operation on schedule. The ICC detention fines of 1973 at Corwith meant that something would have to happen sooner than that to avoid serious legal problems. Santa Fe's operating department was looking for a way out but could not see any until the day in late 1974 that a Univac salesman named John Simmons walked into the office of William Paul, special assistant to Santa Fe's vice president of operations and head of the Operations Research Group.

Simmons wanted to present a new concept in data processing: a software package from Univac called *RPS 418* (*R*eport *P*rocessing *S*ystem for the Univac 418 computer) that would allow the users to create their own applications programs if system-support people would generate file space for them. RPS was incredibly crude by today's standards, but Bill Paul saw what could become a whole new way of processing information. If ISD could not provide programmers for three years, perhaps operating people could be trained quickly enough to get Corwith out of trouble.

Executives from ISD saw demonstrations of RPS in Chicago that fall, but the concept of the users' doing their own applications was so strange that they really could not fathom what Univac and Bill Paul were suggesting. The fact that RPS was so rudimentary perhaps made the necessary imaginative leap too great a feat for pragmatic men. The Corwith project remained an idea and a need for the rest of 1974.

During the fall demonstrations, Univac-Chicago had assigned another salesman, Joe Bradway. Bradway had the most unusual combination of qualities for a salesman: being truly sincere in trying to meet the customers needs and projecting that sincerity while having the salesmanship of an ace used-car dealer. These unique personality traits had much to do with the success of the MAPPER OX project, just as did Bill Paul's ability to see possibilities beyond the rudimentary capabilities of RPS. In fact, a chance combination of several unusual personalities were critical to the project's success since it took an unusual view of the world to see the potential for user-developed computer systems.

After the RPS demonstrations, Bradway began to see if something else would do better than RPS. While visiting the Univac Plant at Roseville, Minnesota, he had seen the plant running on a system developed there by the operating people at the plant. Perhaps a system built by operating people for their own needs would appeal to other operating people, even if the operations were for completely different businesses.

The end result of this was that Bradway first mentioned the name "MAPPER" to a Santa Fe employee, Steve Anderson, over lunch at Chicago's Quarterback Club in January of 1975. Anderson had been in operations research until the year before and had spent the last three months of 1974 at Corwith as a trainee getting field experience before returning to the freight-train operations section of Santa Fe's transportation department. His first assignment at Corwith had been, "Look at the paperwork problem and fix it!" As an electrical-engineering student, Anderson had learned Fortran from a one-quarter course and had been doing Fortran timesharing for cash-flow analysis in operations research. This small exposure to data processing and an even smaller exposure to Corwith's problems had convinced him that the only solution was a computer system, even if he had to program it himself in Fortran.

The RPS demonstrations had fit right in with this belief. Bradway's description of MAPPER as a far more flexible and efficient RPS was reported to Bill Paul. Lawrence Cena, then vice president of operations, was persuaded to let Anderson and Jim Shepard of the Corwith committee, who had also seen the RPS demonstrations, go to Roseville and sit down with the inventors of MAPPER. A simple track-switching application would be coded on MAPPER and demonstrated to ISD people to show the feasibility of letting the operating department take care of its own needs at Corwith. This had the great advantage of letting ISD concentrate on the Barstow system, which looked like it would just meet its 1976 deadline.

Anderson and Shepard fit into the unusual personality category just as did Bradway and Paul. Their minimal DP experience made them so naive about what could not be done that they never realized how much MAPPER would have to grow to be able to handle a railroad yard's operations in real-time. By the time they realized that MAPPER needed a large amount of development time itself, they were sure that it could be done. Part of this attitude came from some other unusual personalities, Lou Schlueter, Chuck Hanson, Bill Gray, and Lynn Mielke of Univac, who seemed to make changes in MAPPER so easily when and as requested, that Anderson and Shepard saw no reason to think anything was impossible. The degree of faith required to propose MAPPER as a real possibility seemed more appropriate to seminary students than to railroad operations researchers.

The demonstration of the test MAPPER application was April 10, 1975, at Roseville. The operations representative, Don Ruegg, who later became vice president of operations when Cena moved to the presidency, was highly impressed. The ISD representatives pointed out, and rightly so based on their experience, that MAPPER would eat the computer alive if a large transaction volume were attempted. Since Santa Fe was an all-IBM shop in those days, they could see no reason to take on an unproven software system based on a radical concept and do it on a strange vendor's equipment to boot.

Several months later IBM's "Data Management System" (DMS) was proposed as ISD's answer to MAPPER and the need for user programming. When combined with the need to learn all about a new vendor if MAPPER were adopted, the counterproposal was accepted by management in August. A group of four people were formed into the "OX Committee": Shepard and Anderson plus Tino Langfeld, a management trainee just graduating from the operations-research schooling period, and W. Dave Thomson, the agent or head clerical supervisor at Corwith, who certainly knew what the problems were. The name "OX" was Bill Paul's acronym for "Operations Xpeditor" since the aim of the OX project was to put the Corwith committee report into effect and hopefully speed up railroad operations.

Through the fall of 1975, the group trained and attempted to start developing simple yard applications. DMS in those days was in its newborn stage, highly unstable and requiring a great deal of file-handling programming from ISD to do simple tasks. Even though MAPPER was hardly more advanced than that stage itself, at least in the programmed-application area, it at least was stable and required only ISD's system support instead of both that and applications I/O support. The upshot was that operations demanded and got the smallest possible computer to run MAPPER, a used 1106, in a meeting just before Thanksgiving, 1975. MAPPER/OX was approved, if only as an research-and-development project.

In the time before the first terminals were installed in the old accounting room on the second floor of the Corwith terminal building, the OX group went through the first classes held for MAPPER coordinators. Since the 1106 would not be installed at Topeka before April of 1976, the group's terminals were connected over telephone lines to the Roseville development system so that work could begin, which occurred February 4, 1976.

With a large amount of administrative and planning duties to be covered by Shepard and Thomson, Anderson and Langfeld were the only members actually coding in MAPPER. To get more local participation, two members of the Corwith staff were loaned to the OX group: W. Spencer Seery, who was an assistant agent or immediate clerical supervisor, and Steve George, a supervisor of transportation. Seery and Anderson began to develop a simple TOFC billing application on April Fool's Day. Univac too pitched in with technical help, assigning Bill Ficken, an expert in MAPPER internals who could help the Santa Fe system-support people in Topeka through the CRTs.

The master plan of attack followed the strategy but not the details of the Corwith report. The Corwith committee had pointed out that the railroad waybill was the source of information for all other records so that it should be the first task completed, and then its information could be used as the basis for yard, piggyback, and central-system reports. However, MAPPER's flexibility made the card-oriented information layouts an actual hindrance, so the same data elements were used but in entirely different arrangements. Shepard, who had been on the Corwith committee, convinced everyone that billing indeed should be first, followed by the yard, and then piggyback. In the end, the whole system would be interlocked so any update to one of the modules automatically updated any other affected parts. This three-way arrangement was the first of its kind in the industry.

Univac had originally designed MAPPER as a series of manual functions, planning only for minimal use of the programming language then available, RBG. RBG was simply a means to string together manual functions and call them as a single command. The largest RBG at the Roseville plant was 22 functions strung together. By early June, Seery and Anderson had the billing RBG ready with 302 functions. Clerks began training and testing the new programs at that time, and numerous holes were discovered simply because the Roseville plant had never permitted the kinds of demands on the system that Santa Fe had built in. Ficken plus W. Gene Perry and his staff on Santa Fe system-support people at Topeka were kept busy designing and testing fixes to the system problems the new billing RBGs had uncovered.

The first live trial of the billing system occurred the week of June 14. The relative slowness of RBG, since each function was just a stored screen of what the manual function would have looked like, slowed the billing down too much during the critical evening peak. When coupled with the unfamiliarity of the clerks with CRT processing, Shepard made the decision to revert to the old manual system after five days.

The new plan was to try again in a month. Meanwhile the system-support people were working on better ways to handle file updates, and Anderson was sent to Roseville to talk about the possibility of a faster and more flexible language than RPG. Hanson and Mielke, the MAPPER internals programmers at Roseville, had been toying with something called RPX (for Report Processing Experimental) for just that purpose. The obvious mutual need for Santa Fe to succeed on the next attempt at Corwith spurred everyone, though RPX was not ready for production until several months later.

With better training and a few system fixes to avoid such disasters as deadly embraces in core, the second attempt, beginning July 19, was a success. After a week of operation, and most important, getting through the big Friday-night TOFC rush, the old billing typewriters were stored in the office basement for good. Since the piggyback business was growing a little each week, and there were no layoffs at all because of the computer, the clerks began to accept the system as a lot easier way to beat the second-shift TOFC rush. In a month's time, "The UNIVAC," as the clerks called it, was just another part of the office, except that coffee or cokes spilled on the keyboard caused a whole lot more problems than if the typewriters were still there. Progress always has a few drawbacks!

There were lots of little fixes to cover small problems in the applications RBGs. But the real effort was in two areas after the system's first success. The most pressing problem was that RBG was still too slow and ate up far too much I/O power. The next big part of the applications planned to be brought up was the trainyard system, which kept an inventory of every railroad car and its yard location. It was obvious the 1106 could not handle the yard system with RBG. So Roseville rushed hard to get RPX ready to run at the Santa Fe. Several more times, Santa Fe people made the journey to Roseville to convert their RBGs into the new RPX language so that Hanson and Mielke could test their inventions under the Santa Fe's heavy load.

This began a trend that lasts to this day, that every release of MAPPER has one or two small holes that only Santa Fe can find because its usage is so immense.

The other big push was in getting MAPPER to communicate to the existing IBM-teletype system so that the paper-tape reportings could be abolished. The two manufacturers had assiduously avoided developing a way to communicate with each other because of competitive rivalries. Santa Fe could not accept that as an answer so Ficken and other Univac people began to develop a bisynchronous protocol to get OX and the teletype teleprocessing system, known as "TP," to talk to each other. When the new communications system became operational late in 1976, the clerks really accepted the OX system because the preparation and transmission of the paper-tape data reports to the TP computer was the most hated job in the office. No matter how threatening the computer was to their jobs, they could not ignore the fact that it had banished much of the drudge work.

During this time there was much apprehension about the effects of the OX project on the regular DP department. Barstow yard had been turned on live as scheduled, but there was as yet no effort under way to link the planned ISD billing/accounting system to the Barstow yard programs. Each part of the railroad had an ISD fieldman assigned, called the "input supervisor," who was responsible for making sure the TP reports were prompt and accurate. The input supervisor at Corwith was Bill Cox, then less than a year on the job. Corwith, among its many other problems, had for years had the worst error rate on data inputted to the TP system of any station on the railway. While the best large stations were running 0.3 error rates, Corwith's often was over ten times larger. Cox was asked to make sure that the Corwith error rate did not get worse and to relay reports of how effective OX really was.

What had not been counted on was that a bright, young input supervisor would see how easy it was to make MAPPER do what he needed to reduce the error rate. Cox was given a sign-on to the OX system and proceeded to develop one of the first new RPXs, which had been renamed "RUN." This RUN was called "TRAUTO" because it automatically sent the old TP reports from MAPPER. Cox began to do most of his work on MAPPER, as did all his successors in later years. By the time the whole OX system of waybilling, yard, and piggyback modules was installed, Cox's successor was enjoying a 0.2 error rate, best on the railroad and fifteen times better than before MAPPER.

With the arrival of the RUN language tape in November, the billing RPGs were converted to RUN language, and work on the yard system progressed rapidly. The day the new tape arrived, so did Charley Hoover, a clerk from San Francisco and a former doctoral student in romance languages. Seery had become an exceptionally good RUN designer, and he too had been a doctoral student in language studies. The same pattern occurred with Hoover, and a very large share part of the existing OX system is based on his work. Since Langfeld had become involved with training the clerks and handling people problems, Hoover, Seery, Cox, and Anderson were the only programmers of the OX system. The yard module was turned on in January, 1977, and after Seery was promoted to manager of the piggyback yard in May, the remaining three designed and implemented the piggyback system at the piggyback yard in August that year. This computerized TOFC system was the first anywhere and was running over two years before even the most rudimentary TOFC system was ready anywhere else.

When the van system was installed, almost every single clerical function at Corwith had been computerized. The applications team, never more than four full-time people, started April 1, 1976, and had a billing, yard, and TOFC system running by September 1, 1977. Not one of the group had any formal DP training, other than Anderson's one-quarter class in Fortran. For comparison, ISD had needed up to twenty full-time programmers working in assembly language for two years to come up with the yard system alone at Barstow. There was no difference in the abilities of the two groups, the only real difference was that MAPPER was available. Just the sheer ease of coding MAPPER helped enormously, but there was another effect that was at least as important. Since MAPPER needed only very few applications people, the OX group never had to contend with the administrative and bureaucratic hindrances that the larger Barstow group faced. The net effect was that 100 percent of the OX programmer's time could be spent programming in a very productive way. MAPPER's ability to allow a true team approach to very large projects accounts for at least half of its great productivity.

Before the van system was installed, a second 1106 had been required. There were no other 1106 multiprocessors, so Perry's system-support group had to fight that battle for some time before it ran smoothly. Los Angeles billing came up live in January, 1978, and the Corwith success was repeated. The TP waybill extracts had become an even worse problem there with the expansion in piggyback service that had occurred since Corwith billing started a year and a half before. Los Angeles in January, 1978, was handling more TOFC than Corwith in July, 1976. By the time of the OX billing implementation, the waybill extracts were one week, or 2,000 records, behind at any one time and getting worse. Within five minutes after the implementation, the new extracts were completely current and the backlog was cleaned up in six days.

Corwith was seeing the same kind of TOFC growth that Los Angeles experienced. Between July, 1976, and the end of 1978, the TOFC traffic at Corwith doubled. Because of MAPPER/OX, no additional clerks were required.

One of the ways that OX became acceptable to line management was by handling requests for special reports and emergency program changes as quickly as possible. Whereas ISD required a formal project application, or "PA," to be handled through regular channels, the average OX supervisor could run functions at his local yard to get special information. If the comlexity of a request went beyond his ability, one of the OX group could get it for him very quickly, often within minutes, rather than weeks or months as the old PA system required.

The most spectacular example of this occurred during a clerks' strike in the fall of 1978. Santa Fe's car-distribution offices at Kansas City and Barstow receive shipper requests for empty railcars to load. By the time of the strike, OX yard stations had RUNs that allowed the car distributors to be notified automatically that empty cars were available at Corwith or wherever OX yard was implemented. The distributor could match car orders with car availability and use another RUN to direct the empty car where the order was. The manager of car utilization, Mel Brewer, was manning the Kansas City office during the strike, and Steve Anderson was sent there to act as a clerk. Since the strike stopped nearly all train service, Brewer got to talking to Anderson during the lulls about the trouble he was having getting some of his PAs programmed by ISD. Before the strike was over four days later, OX had the capabilities requested in the PAs, and Brewer canceled them because they were no longer necessary. Shortly thereafter, one of the clerks at Corwith most interested in the computer was added to the transportation staff as a full-time RUN designer since Brewer had seen how easily new functions could be added.

Other departments had begun to see advantages in using the OX data base to generate some of their own reports. Marketing people especially liked the up-to-date TOFC information that could be gotten by shipper name or by trailer type or by destination or by almost anything at all. The ability to look at data in unforeseen ways made the inevitable special requests very, very much easier to handle.

The accounting department could see even more uses. They formed their own group of RUN designers in early 1979 and began to create bills and reports directly from OX yard information. Previously, OX had just automated preparation of various reports, which had to be rekeyed in the three regional accounting offices. The new methods began to handle this information directly without rekeying.

Once in a while, there would be some semantic problems. One Friday morning, one of the accounting group fired up a new program that ran for one hour, fourteen minutes and affected system response. When the new RUN was pinpointed as the cause of the slowdown, the OX group noticed that the coder's inexperience made it somewhat inefficient. When questioned as to whether his new RUN was coded as efficiently as it could be, his answer was that of course it was efficient. It took only an hour and a quarter to do the work of three typists and two clerks working for a month! How much more efficient did it have to be?

An even more important function was the abolition of the "turtles." Larry Cena had moved from operations to become president of the railroad, and he considered the postmen who carried billing information from the yards to the accounting offices to be as slow as turtles. Based on an idea from Dave Thomson, who used to work in the old Corwith accounting ofice, Bill Cox and the accounting group in ISD invented "RCAOTAPE TRANSFER," which each night copies all the prior day's OX billing onto tape. This tape was then reloaded and fed to the IBM system, which ran the new central accounting office in Topeka. Again a great deal of rekeying was avoided, and the improvement in cash flow was tremendous. As OX billing and RCAOTAPE spread across the railroad, the turtles approached extinction.

This kind of growth eventually forced the OX group to expand and change structure. Charley Hoover moved back to the West Coast to work on OX with the operating department there but still acted in concert with the OX group in Chicago. As more and more stations came under OX, the old method of handling trouble in the middle of the night (roust one of the OX group out of bed) became impossible. In April, 1978, four "supervisors of system reliability" began manning telephones at Topeka around the clock to handle problems and walk new clerks through procedural problems. (It should be noted that the instructions for the programs were right on each screen, but new clerks were often so in awe of the computer that they forgot to read them!) In early 1979, a former Railroad Line Superintendent, Mike Haverty, took charge of OX for the operating department and formed "operating systems" out of the OX group and the data-integrity group in ISD that, among other things, was in charge of the input supervisors across the railroad.

The reliability group brought in some much-needed experts in documentation, implementation, and training. Each of Santa Fe's three operating grand divisions was assigned a pair of three-man teams of implementers to spread OX across the railroad faster. Classrooms were set up that contained more CRTs than were at Corwith for the first implementation so that new RUN designers could be trained (each implementer had to pass the course) and to train agency people before OX was installed at their yard. Again MAPPER's flexibility made the training easier since "backup" MAPPER systems could run in the computer side by side with the live system. The trainees on the backup system could use data from real yard operations of the previous day without changing any live information.

Obviously, the load on the computer was increasing almost daily. Whenever a RUN designer saw that a new function could save processing power, a request was made to the local Univac system-support people, who might pass it on to Roseville but more often did it themselves. Once the new function proved out on the Santa Fe, Roseville was talked into including it on the next release of MAPPER so that Santa Fe's system could be as close to Univac standard as possible. This was just an extension of the process that had produced the RUN language itself and fit right in with the shared attitudes at both Santa Fe and Univac-Roseville—everyone's aim was to make things better and faster whenever and however possible. With the anitbureaucratic attitude that had gotten MAPPER going first in Univac and then in Santa Fe, attaining these goals was something that just seemed to happen naturally. The same process occurred within Santa Fe for the RUN coding.

Of course, the load was bound to grow faster than these efficiency improvements so a bigger CPU, an 1100/82, had been installed in 1979 with two more on order. Even so, there were severe performance problems on the larger system in the fall of that year. The "can-do" attitude of both Univac and Santa Fe saved the day. After several months of suffering, Gene Perry's support people and the Univac support people under Roy Kretzinger discovered that the old update-file allocations were fine when the CPU was the restriction, but now the 1100/82 had so much power that the I/O distribution was killing the response time. Rather than blame the applications RUN designers, they kept looking and fixing until an algorithm for spreading the I/Os evenly across all storage devices was invented. The response returned to the several-second level that everyone had become used to, and as usual, the next release of MAPPER incorporated the "spread code" for all MAPPER users.

One interesting sidelight to the response problem is how it highlighted people's changing expectations. The very best typists at Corwith could make one TOFC waybill in about one to two minutes. The preparation and transmission of the TP extracts required one to two minutes more per waybill, and typing a new punchcard for the manual card inventory took another half-minute. The average time to do all of this in MAPPER was about thirty to forty seconds, including time for the clerk to look at the information to be typed and type it on the abbreviated screen. Actual processing time included in those totals was usually only four to ten seconds, which was the only part affected when the response time slowed down before invention of the spread code. If that time now went to twenty seconds, the clerks simply could not tolerate such ridiculously slow response, even though they were still minutes better per waybill than in the old days.

Another interesting system-support problem was MAPPER's need for purge. Each day, the system had to be taken off-line and the updates and files rearranged for a new day's work. This had been no problem at the Univac plant, where only two shifts were worked, leaving midnight to 7 A.M.

for purge and computer maintenance. Railroads unfortunately have to run twenty-four hours a day, seven days a week. And, as the size of the OX data base grew, so did the purge time till it required more than one and a half hours per day. During this time, the clerks could not work, which greatly cut into the efficiency gains that OX was installed for. Numerous patches were tried, but finally Roseville realized how serious the problem was and worked with Topeka to invent "Purge On The Fly," which reorganized the files without taking the system down. This saved incredible amounts of time in the field, so much so that the clerks in the field can now expect their CRTs to be ready an average of 99 percent of the time.

The new purgeless operation had an interesting side-effect because it not only cut management complaints from the field about excessive purge time but also reduced all other complaints. Apparently, if the computer is available whenever needed, other minor problems are not nearly so irritating. This effect, like the response-time effect, leads to the conclusion that a system like MAPPER operates in an environment that demands more than real-time performance. Perhaps "unreal-time" better describes the demands put on a system like MAPPER/OX.

By mid-1981, the original 1106 had been upgraded to four 1100/82 CPUs with another two on order. About 75 percent of the TP records scheduled for conversion were on OX, including over 90 percent of the billing. The rollcall of Santa Fe yards covered by OX sound like a who's who of the sunbelt: Part of Kansas City, Topeka, Wichita, Oklahoma City, Dallas/Fort Worth, Houston, Galveston, Amarillo, Albuquerque, Denver, El Paso, Phoenix, Flagstaff, San Diego, Los Angeles, Bakersfield, Fresno, Stockton, Oakland, San Francisco, and, as the old railroad station announcers used to say, all points in between. Even the Santa Fe's wholly owned subsidiary, the Toledo, Peoria, and Western runs on OX as its trains cover central Illinois from Fort Madison, Iowa to Effner, Indiana.

Complete coverage should happen in the fall of 1982. At that time, the system will consist of about 2,000 CRTs and 800 printers or so, which are all connected to the central site at Topeka through Santa Fe's privately owned microwave network. The disk storage will hold nearly 30 billion characters in 32 model 8450 disk drives per 1100/84 (a 4×4 multiprocess consisting of two of the 1100/82s). In the ultimate system, users will call 420,000 RUNs per day that will process 60 million I/Os and 600 million report lines.

Since the up-time that the user sees is usually in the 98-99 percent range (the actual Santa Fe target is 98.5 percent or better), backup to MAPPER has not really been a problem. There are a few places, though, such as Checkpoint Chico at the entrance to Corwith's piggyback yard, where any outage is an outrage. One way this has been handled is that UTS-400 microprocessors, which use the Intel 8080 8-bit computer-on-a-chip, were programmed to act as a frontend to MAPPER. The data entered on the screen is edited for reasonableness by the 400 and sent on to MAPPER in compressed format. But should MAPPER's polling stop, the 400 realizes the fact and automatically stores the data off to diskette. When MAPPER returns, the 400 again senses the change and automatically begins sending the data to MAPPER in the sequence it was stored. The user sees none of this. The 400 can operate on the Dartmouth "Basic" language and so acts as a local personal computer for certain applications that may or may not need to talk to MAPPER. These capabilities are just extra benefits since the six terminals off each 400 processor provide a very cost-effective peripheral arrangement for MAPPER.

With the OX project's great size, the people structure inevitably got larger, but the basic end-user orientation is still alive. The Systems-Reliability Group became part of Santa Fe's Network Management Center and trebled in size. The original four RUN designers became a group of ten under operating systems who maintain the current 700+ RUNs for the operating department and handle improvements on an informal basis. There are permanent groups of RUN designers in quality control and accounting, while the marketing, communications, and personnel departments have trained people who do considerable amounts of work on OX. Bill Paul has since become the vice president of the information-systems department, and Jim Shepard is the head of a part of ISD called "Client Relations" that has been created to do nothing but deal with users. Bill Cox's job in client relations is to work with the other departments to help them design their MAPPER applications in the most efficient way possible, though he normally does not do the actual coding of the RUN. The TP system is now being rewritten, and there is a group within ISD development that works exclusively on making over the OX-TP interface, though they still work in conjunction with operating systems so that the new procedures will not be at cross-purposes with user needs.

Even though the original group has now expanded ten times, the same almost magical breakthroughs in user problems still occur. The MAPPER-trained people in marketing are required each year to publish a source book for sales people in the field that shows Santa Fe's largest customers, what they ship, whether their Santa Fe volume is shrinking or growing, and so on. This used to be a three-month project with the word-processing services, what with corrections, additions, and just the necessity for having someone else type up and assemble several hundred pages of information. This has been done on MAPPER since 1980, and the annual updates take about a week.

During a demonstration of the OX system to a dignitary from a foreign railroad, the visitor asked how long it had taken to develop the printout program. The marketing man replied that it took far too long, about four hours. If he had known what he was doing, it really should have been done in thirty minutes! The visitor, who was used to the standard process of making a formal request, getting a priority assigned, and then waiting several months for information that was needed immediately, was most suitably impressed.

Another example of the continuing user orientation and flexibility came from the operating department. Each of the Santa Fe's grand divisions has former agency people assigned to watch over the agency operations for that territory, as station supervisors. Naturally, the eastern-lines people head-quartered at Topeka were working on a daily basis with ISD, so that it was inevitable that they would pick up on some of ISD's concerns about MAPPER/ OX. When the first eastern-lines installation beyond Topeka was planned for Oklahoma City, there was a great deal of resistance on their part, especially as they compared it to the Barstow system that had been copied into Santa Fe's huge humpyard at Kansas City in 1977.

Some of the problems they mentioned were Corwith and San Francisco special features that really did not fit Oklahoma City, and so the OX group worked over several years to keep integrating the eastern-lines suggestions into OX. As one of them prepared to retire in 1982, he commented to a member of the original OX group that he knew he had opposed the OX system at the beginning, but now he was convinced it really was a fine way to run a railroad. The fact that Seery's operating-systems group was continuing to accept suggestions and get the changes made without excessive formality was the clinching factor. Things got done faster when an operating person could talk to other operating people to get operating computer problems solved quickly. The station supervisor's praise after his initial opposition was one of the finest compliments OX ever received.

Beyond the completion of the OX project, the grand plan for MAPPER in late 1981 is somewhat fuzzy since the conversion of the TP system is taking the attention of every department. Even so, there are very many ways the existing data could be utilized in new combinations and by other departments. There has been such explosive growth over the six years of the OX project that one of the worst problems has been making sure that potential users realize the volume and variety of data available. The other big problem is that just evolutionary improvements in the existing OX system could easily consume very large amounts of computer power without any big, new projects to make things worse. Explorations of the possibility of a compiler or faster interpreter for MAPPER are underway and, if successful, would easily permit new major applications within the existing hardware. At that time, MAPPER would be the only computer language in the world that could process data at the manual level, as functions run on the basic data, as strung-together functions (RUN), and then once a stable RUN was designed, as a very efficient compiled load module—covering the whole spectrum of real-time data processing with a single language.

As a summary of what the OX project meant to the railway, we can look at a standard measure of efficiency known as revenue-ton-miles/employee-hour. Between 1971 and 1975, the year before OX began, the index improved 13. The railway moved 13 more tons of products in 1975 than in 1971. During the same length of time after OX began, 1976 to 1980, the index went up 28. Santa Fe moved a lot more coal in 1980 than in 1976, and there were the cumulative effects of many small improvements, but some significant part of that doubling of the rate of improvement was because of OX.

21 GTE Automatic Electric Operations, Management, and MAPPER

Neil Biteler

GTE Automatic Electric Environment

Let me give you a little background about my company. I work for GTE Automatic Electric in Northlake, Illinois. At Northlake we have some 2 million square feet under one roof with approximately 6,000 employees, and we manufacture electronic telephone switching equipment. In our data-processing center, we have over $30 million in data equipment.

To give you a further picture of our operations, my particular project took place in early October in 1977. Late in 1976, we had a long strike, and during that strike, our schedules were not adjusted. So we were working off a very large backlog. As we anticipated 1978, we could see that marketing was forecasting significant growth and major introductions of new products. In fact, there were three new product lines scheduled for start-up in 1978, from our small 120-line systems, all the way up to our 4600-line office systems.

In our factory we normally had 100,000 printed wiring assemblies on the shop floor. It is a dynamic environment where three hundred orders hit each week. Each order ranges in lot size from one to two hundred cards for a total schedule of 20,000. We were already seeing a minimum of fifty to sixty mandatory change orders a week released into work-in-process.

There were forty people working three shifts, seven days per week, trying to control the operation, and failing. To top it off, we were looking forward to a material-resource planning (MRP) system cutover in mid-1978.

Management gave me the directive: Get a real-time shop-floor control system on line in ninety days! Control the shop floor while we work off the backlog, and debug the MRP system! Design the system, install it on the fly, with no increase in costs. *Period*!

This chapter has been excerpted from an address delivered by Neil Biteler, the manager of manufacturing operations analysis, GTE Automatic Electric, Northlake, Illinois. The address was entitled "Operations Management View" and was presented at the Information Management Conference for Manufacturing in Chicago, Illinois, November 18-20, 1980. Reprinted with permission.

The Approach to the Problem

We first had to evaluate our alternatives:

> We interviewed thirteen vendors in approximately ten days.
>
> Within two weeks, we had selected the most promising solutions and, ultimately, chose a system called MAPPER that Sperry Univac offered.
>
> We signed a contract within thirty days of getting the assignment.

We are not talking about a mini. We are talking about a main-frame computer, completely dedicated to getting control of printed wiring-card-assembly manufacture, the guts of our business.

What Is MAPPER?

> It is a nonprocedural report-processing system.
>
> It is user oriented.
>
> It is CRT accessed.
>
> It has real-time updating capability.

Some MAPPER Strengths

> It has the ability for the users to inquire or input data.
>
> It has simple commands such as search, sort, and totalize.
>
> It allows the users to create their own reports, and there is no need for outside programming help. *The users do it themselves*!
>
> Changes in the system are easy to make.
>
> The system has effective controls for monitoring resource utilization.

Systems Design

As to the question of approaching the systems design, I got together with my boss and some of the key operations people. We went to the blackboard one Saturday morning, and we wrote the spec for the system. It simply said:

We wanted to know the status of assembly on a real-time basis.

We wanted to know what was short and what was being done about it.

We wanted the ability to view the various support operations such as purchasing, receiving, and card fabrication and to get promises for those things that were constraining assembly operations.

We would use our old shop-floor-control batch system which had a keypunched-card packet for each basket as a base to build on.

Our orders are broken down into basket increments of ten to twenty card assemblies. Each basket has a deck of cards. Each time that basket moves from area 1 to area 2, that area 1 card is pulled and run through a card reader. In the old batch system, the work-in-process reports were three inches thick and were run over night. In our new system, these same cards are picked up and read into the computer every hour or two.

Since time was of the essence, we took every shortcut available to us. Once we had the specification, we knew what was required to control the environment. We drafted three people from the operations staff and one from materials management:

One operations analyst

Two industrial engineers

One systems analyst (a long-service employee who had designed some of the older systems)

A young financial analyst with an MBA

None of these people had ever been involved in programming or design work such as we were attempting with MAPPER, but we all understood the operation and what the operating people wanted in a system.

We then stripped the data from the IBM system to build the MAPPER data base.

We extracted the data through RUN (RPG) designs, a simple kind of programming that the users could do.

We formated all of our reports just like the old reports being done manually. This meant no relearning for the production-control team.

Auditing the People's System Competence

Before turning the system on, we had to audit the people's ability to use the system. To do this, we:

Designed special training courses and then provided on-line exams to test their level of competence since most of those who use the system have no education beyond the high school level.

We certified who would go on the system by exams. To arouse interest, we also created our own PR material, one called the *MAPPER NEWS*, to involve people who use the system by relating successes that they experienced and to recognize their contributions.

Audit and Control of Operations and Materials Management

The data that we had in the MAPPER data bases:

Mapper Data Base

Open orders (daily)

Stock-process system: shortages (daily)

Stock status (daily)

Stock location (daily)

Operation Labor hours (monthly)

Audits and Controls we put into effect

Audits/Controls

Report Card

Input/Output

Dispatch lists

Staging audit

Age audit

Priority control

Holds: engineering

Test-method changes

Labor-efficiency report

Budget analysis

Table 21-1 is a daily input/output report, and you can see here where each area is identified. It indicates how much they got that day, their week-to-date input, as well as their week-to-date output, and their current inventory broken down into: ahead, current, and behind. This is a document that would come to the operations manager's desk each morning.

The hot list (table 21-2) defines the particular part numbers that each department is currently short. You will see here there are several areas.

Area 5 has 27 percent of the cards that are currently needed to satisfy these demands; that's the department nearest the door, nearest completion.

Table 21-1
Daily: Input/Output

	AREA 0		AREA 9	
WEEK	1133		1133	
SCHEDULE	17660		17660	

	AREA 0		AREA 9	
	DAY	WTD	DAY	WTD
INPUT				
AHEAD	0	0	240	240
CURRENT	0	0	668	668
BEHIND	0	0	78	78
750-RP	0	0	0	0
CONV-RP	0	0	0	0
TOTAL	0	0	986	986
OUTPUT				
AHEAD	50	50	15	15
CURRENT	0	0	420	420
BEHIND	23	23	1130	1130
750-RP	0	0	0	0
CONV-RP	0	0	0	0
TOTAL	73	73	1565	1565
INVENTORY				
AHEAD	34488		225	
CURRENT	6660		6876	
BEHIND	1710		35186	
750-RP	0		0	
CONV-RP	364		0	
TOTAL	43222		42287	

Table 21-2
Hot List

PART NUMBER PR	BASE	SUFF ISS	TEST TYPE	DEPT 120	DEPT 300	6SEM CS57	DEPT 750	DEPT 652	TOTAL QTY	QTY INSTK	NET REQRD	TOTAL AVAIL
FB	020889	A	T2	0	0	0	0	3	3	0		0
FB	020903	A	No. T.T	130	0	0	0	0	130	0		325
FB	020913	A	T2	0	48	200	0	0	248	11		649
KH	840129	A60A	G1	0	0	0	1	0	1	0		31
KH	840137	A60A	G1	0	0	0	3	0	3	1		38
KH	840198	3A0B	P1	0	0	0	0	33	33			0
KH	840211	3A0A	E1	0	0	2	0	0	2			0

TOTAL ENTRIES - 273

NET REQRD	TOTAL AVAIL
2343 —	27.8%**
454 —	5.4%
84 —	1.0%
1571 —	18.6%
494 —	5.9%
545 —	6.5%
2027 —	24.1%
108 —	1.3%
8428 —	100.0%

TOTAL SHORTAGE

			AVAILABLE ON SHOP FLOOR	
DEPT 120	=	1526	AREA 5	=
DEPT 180	=	4	AREA 8	=
DEPT 182	=	1286	AREA 4	=
DEPT 300	=	352	AREA 3	=
6SEM CS57	=	4501**	AREA 2	=
DEPT 750	=	447	AREA 1	=
DEPT 652	=	137	AREA 9	=
SPEC SPL	=	0	AREA 0	=
470 & 05	=	255	TOTAL	—
TOTAL QTY	=	8508		

From the priority list (table 21-2) we go to the dispatcher (table 21-3). This is the list that he gets that shows by part number the A and B priority items, what to run first. In the age audit (table 21-4) we highlight jobs over sixty days old on the shop floor. It details those jobs and their status to the operations manager as a weekly exception control. Inaccurate data is also purged in this way.

Table 21-5 is our staging audit. We can tell what particular department is constraining production. You can see there are 7,300 cards that are short one last item. Three thousand are being held up for purchased parts, another 1,800 for the fabricated card itself.

The Weekly Report Card

We give the operations manager a ten-week horizon to help him see trends. It has been abbreviated in these examples (tables 21-6 and 21-7), but you can see

The schedule

The input

The output

The inventory on the shop floor

Our ahead- or behind-schedule position

Inventory on hold

The technical-service holds

Engineering change-order holds

Delays in the area (it tells how much of that inventory is more than twenty-eight days old)

Also we track:

The number of printed wiring card assemblies that were picked complete in the pick week. You can see we were only getting 53 percent of the material that was planned to be available in week 1101. (I can tell you this was a ten-week high.)

Compare the weekly report card, before and after one hundred weeks of MAPPER system control!

Table 21-3
Dispatch List

PR	PART NUMBER BASE	SUFF	ISS	ORDER NUMBER	BKT NO	P R	BKT QTY	NUM BKT	ORDER QTY	REQD WEEK
FB	015003	A	005	661146	023	A	008	032	00250	1116
FB	015003	A	005	717175	003	A	008	109	00150	1124
FB	015006	A	004	641618	005	A	008	007	00050	1114
FB	015058	A	006	670693	001	A	010	001	00010	1132
FB	015207	A	008	634609	001	A	005	001	00005	1127
FB	015623	A	002	653024	001	A	007	001	00007	1128
FB	020090	A	005	614287	001	A	001	001	00001	1666
FB	020777	A	003	699070	001	A	014	5	00030	1120
FB	020831	A	003	640498	002	A	014	008	00111	1129
FB	015045	A	001	646604	001	B	007	001	00007	1129
FB	015551	A	003	646786	001	B	008	001	00008	1130
FB	015589	A	002	622194	002	B	028	004	00108	1126
FB	015589	A	002	622194	003	B	028	004	00108	1126
FB	015635	A	006	648014	013	B	009	013	00177	1113
FB	015701	A	001	641762	001	B	005	001	00005	1113

Table 21-4
Age Audit

	DAYS =	0-5	6-10	11-20	21-30	31-60
AREA 0	NUMBER OF CARDS	0	8068	9189	3809	497
AREA 1	NUMBER OF CARDS	6175	456	637	24	4
AREA 2	NUMBER OF CARDS	2935	264	141	12	3
AREA 3	NUMBER OF CARDS	4712	1344	1459	379	346

PR	PART NUMBER BASE	SUFF	ISS	ORDER NUMBER	BRK NO	P R	BRK QTY	NUM BRK	ORDER QTY	REQD WEEK	AR EA	AREA DATE	TOT DAY	TEST TYPE
FB	010016	A	011	629725	004		006	007	00150	1206	3	800813	89	SCATS
FB	010433	1A	003	718113	023	C	005	050	00250	1201	3	800818	84	EMCTS
FB	015003	A	005	625379	009		008	019	00150	1206	3	800819	83	PWR SUP
FB	015004	A	004	625380	001		008	013	00100	1209	3	800819	83	PWR SUP

Table 21-5
Staging Audit

DEP. NO.	DEPARTMENT DESCRIPTION	(LAST) SHORT CARDS	LAST % HELD
030	METAL FINISHING	89	1.2%
060	SPRING CONTACTING	87	1.2%
061	TERMINAL BLOCK ASSEMBLY	0	0.0%
070	PWCA FABRICATION	1843 ——→	25.2%
090	IRON WORK	12	0.2%
105	HQA RELAYS	420	5.8%
140	MISC. ASSEMBLY	159	2.2%
230		50	0.7%
240	PLATING & POLISHING	153	2.1%
300	REG. SEND. & MISC. ELECTRONIC	14	0.2%
487	HYBRIDS-HTV, LABS, BRKVL, LENKR	722	9.9%
604		1	0.0%
640	MISC. PARTS—GENOA	378	5.2%
785		6	0.1%
789		0	0.0%
790	HAND INSERTION	0	0.0%
792		1	0.0%
793	MISC. CORREED ASSEMBLY	104	1.4%
794	SOLDERING & MISC. ASSEMBLY	231	3.2%
799	PWCA ANALYZATION	6	0.1%
860	PURCHASE PARTS	3009 ——→	41.2%
922		18	0.2%
	TOTALS	7303	100.0%

PHYSICAL & COMPUTER STAGING SUMMARY

TOTAL IDENTIFIED CARDS HELD IN PHYSICAL STAGING	7442	
TOTAL RELEASED CARDS WITH 2 OR LESS SHORT	3828	
TOTAL UNRELEASED COMPUTER STAGED CARDS WITH 3 OR MORE SHORT	155	
SUBTOTAL		11425
TOTAL LAST SHORTS BEING PICKED IN PHYSICAL STAGING	1027	
TOTAL CARDS RELEASED/UNRELEASED IN STOCK ROOM PICKABLE	1478	
TOTAL CARDS IN STOCK ROOM WITH NO SPS RECORD	494	
TOTAL CARDS HELD IN PHYSICAL STAGING BREAKDOWN AREA	2020	
SUBTOTAL		5019
TOTAL BEHIND SCHEDULE INPUT	16444	

We have a schedule of 12,000 cards. There are 88,000 in our work-in-process, and only 9,700 of those are behind schedule.

You can see that there are very few cards on hold, in some categories, none. There are only 5,231 cards more than twenty-eight days old, and as far as the picking, we are getting 69 percent complete in the pick week. We are now looking at an inventory value of work-in-process of $3.5 million.

Table 21-6
Before: Weekly Report Card

WEEK NUMBER	1101
PWCA SCHEDULE	14169
INPUT—AHEAD	7103
CURRENT	3376
BEHIND	7283
750-REPAIR	0
CONV-REPAIR	0
TOTAL	17762
OUTPUT—AHEAD	4798
CURRENT	3413
BEHIND	9729
750-REPAIR	411
CONV-REPAIR	737
TOTAL	19088
INVENTORY—AHEAD	76222
CURRENT	16114
BEHIND	139503
750-REPAIR	7002
CONV-REPAIR	3715
TOTAL	242556
AHEAD OF SCHEDULE	12723
BEHIND SCHEDULE	56026
INVENTORY ON HOLD	5102
TECH SERVICES	
0-7 DAYS	2528
8-14 DAYS	2
15-21 DAYS	371
22+ DAYS	892
TOTAL	3793
ECO PENDING	
0-7 DAYS	507
8-14 DAYS	21
15-21 DAYS	0
22+ DAYS	190
TOTAL	718
ECO HOLD	
0-7 DAYS	4
8-14 DAYS	0
15-21 DAYS	0
22+ DAYS	334
TOTAL	338
DELAYS IN AN AREA	
0-7 DAYS	68821
8-14 DAYS	33222
15-21 DAYS	18777
22-28 DAYS	7407
28+ DAYS	34381
SCHEDULED ORDERS % PICKED COMPLETE	53%
INVENTORY VALUE	$10.0 MILLION

STAFFING AT 40 PEOPLE

Table 21-7
After: Weekly Report Card

WEEK NUMBER	1211
PWCA SCHEDULE	11940
INPUT—AHEAD	10014
CURRENT	500
BEHIND	2462
750-REPAIR	0
CONV-REPAIR	75
TOTAL	13051
OUTPUT—AHEAD	591
CURRENT	9026
BEHIND	2459
750-REPAIR	28
CONV-REPAIR	44
TOTAL	12148
INVENTORY—AHEAD	56519
CURRENT	12080
BEHIND	19004
750-REPAIR	96
CONV-REPAIR	388
TOTAL	88087
AHEAD OF SCHEDULE	1275
BEHIND SCHEDULE	9700
INVENTORY ON HOLD	287
TECH SERVICES	
0-7 DAYS	251
8-14 DAYS	32
15-21 DAYS	0
22+ DAYS	0
TOTAL	283
ECO PENDING	
0-7 DAYS	0
8-14 DAYS	0
15-21 DAYS	0
22+ DAYS	0
TOTAL	0
ECO HOLD	
0-7 DAYS	0
8-14 DAYS	0
15-21 DAYS	0
22+ DAYS	4
TOTAL	4
DELAYS IN AN AREA	
0-7 DAYS	39483
8-14 DAYS	19749
15-21 DAYS	11605
22-28 DAYS	3085
28+ DAYS	5231
SCHEDULED ORDERS % PICKED COMPLETE	67%
INVENTORY VALUE	$3.5 MILLION

STAFFING AT 19 PEOPLE

We have gone from approximately $10 million in inventory down to $3.5 million since the system has gone on-line and reduced our manpower to control the three-shift operation from forty to nineteen.

Audit and Control of Data Integrity

There is another facet of auditing control that is very critical and that is *data integrity*.

> With our system, we have user sign-on control to secure the data that is in the computer and control who accesses that data.

> For each new system that is designed, there is an audit designed before the system is released to go on-line.

> There is also a total-systems audit where we audit all of the MAPPER operations on an annual basis.

> Finally, to further secure system integrity, we have a full documentation system where we automatically document our RUN (RPG) designs right on the machine. There are no manual documents. There are no flow diagrams.

Audit and Control of Computer Resource

Since we in manufacturing own our own computer, we do have some other responsibilities for controlling the use of that computer to assure that we are getting optimum machine utilization. We have designed daily monitoring reports that give us indications of how much data we are processing, the timing of tape transfer, and so on.

Each new application is cost justified before it goes into operation. After the application goes on stream, there is an audit in three to nine months after the application is up and running.

Results Achieved

Consider the results. I went out into the factory last week to talk firsthand with the people who are using the system some three years after we started. There is a totally different attitude. People out there feel like they "can do it." The system they have is user oriented. They invented and maintain it. They perform their own periodic audits. What's more, they have stopped fire fighting. They're in *control*.

We protected the long-range strategic plan for systems development.

We have proved that systems can be cost effective by our audit and performance measurements.

One million dollars in annual savings through clerical reductions have been realized through this MAPPER system. You can see we reduced the inventory some $6.5 million.

How many people do we have running it? There is a full-time MAPPER coordinator and one training assistant.

We think MAPPER has a very bright future with our company and are excited about the results achieved!

Conclusion

We did harness a user-oriented report-processing system to audit a system conversion and measure performance of both operations and the materials-management function. Operations management must provide leadership. Data processing is too important to be left to the professionals. A report-processing system can get short-term results quickly and provide the basis for management change too dynamic for a structured system. User confidence in the system is worth more than any audit report. Finally, if we can do it, you can do it!

22 Free Enterprise Computing: In Summary

The full potentials of extensive implementation of the concepts of Free Enterprise Computing are difficult to assess. Clearly, there is a vast flow of information in our society that is not computerized. This is the myriad real-control information elements that run our businesses, operations, and institutions on a minute-to-minute basis. Computerizing this real-control information has important benefits that go far beyond simple productivity improvements over manual paper systems. Expediting and improving the accuracy of the decision-making processes associated with real-control information processing means improving precision and timeliness. This opens up bottlenecks where inventories are held waiting for control decisions to be made. In-process inventories are reduced, and in-process lead times can thereby be drastically shortened. Not only are truly significant productivity gains practical but many benefits are made possible that are difficult to place measurable value on. These added benefits could be of even greater significance in terms of overall impacts.

It is important then that users be enlisted in the control and implementation of computer uses. As one of the users stated, "the control of computer power is too important to be left in the hands of professionals only." Only through effective user involvement in application design and implementation can the productivity and benefits inherent in computer power be disseminated into the areas of real-control in all operations.

The potential and need are enormous. Not only must the armies of users be enlisted, they must be supported by a management that is sensitive to the possible opportunities. Data processing too will have an important role to play as a guide and provider of these utilitarian computer resources to the user-community. Success will depend directly on the degree with which both management and the data-processing professionals support an environment in which Free Enterprise Computing can thrive.

The environment of Free Enterprise Computing is new and different. It has been said that it is not evolutionary but rather revolutionary. Clearly, it is controversial in its nature, especially when viewed by data-processing and auditing establishments that are extensively developed and deeply imbued with the philosophies of the common corporate data base and structured MIS services. The professional personnel resources available to implement these structured approaches to computer services are clearly documented as being insufficient to meet the demands. The computer must now be viewed as what it really is, another tool, and it must be placed in the hands of the users to obtain full potential from its use.

Support from management, data processing, and auditing that nurtures a system-safe, Free Enterprise Computing environment are the essential keys to a successful implementation that can derive full benefits. To provide total freedom for the users without adequate securities and controls would represent a form of computerized anarchy. This cure would be worse than the problems to be remedied. User-oriented systems are now available that are complete and contain capable tools and methods for maintaining security, system safety, and a plan-actual, controlled approach in user application design and implementation.

Knowledgeable, perceptive, sensitive support functions create the truly successful Free Enterprise Computing service environment. *Knowledge* refers to an understanding of the functional processing tools that are available to the users, the security methods and their applicability, and the monitoring and control mechanisms that can ensure proper application implementation according to plan. *Perception* refers to a thorough understanding of real operation needs. This perceptive knowledge will guide the managerial stimulation that will ensure the earliest and broadest possible benefit realization. The *sensitivity* aspect is similar to that associated with the care and nurturing of freedom in a society. A certain faith in the decentralized ability of individuals to best control their immediate operations is also needed in this user-oriented approach to computing. Let the "invisible hand" guide. Avoid a smothering, over control. Instead of attempting to treat the users as recipients of a structured, doled-out computer service, let the adage "Give me a fish, I will eat today. Teach me to fish I will feed myself for the rest of my life" apply to the use of computers also.

Index

About the Author

Louis Schlueter has been with Sperry Univac for over twenty-five years in various technical, system test, engineering, and manufacturing-planning positions. He wrote the initial software design specification for report-processing concepts and was one of the principal initial programmers of the system. He has served as a report-processing systems coordinator for many years. In this capacity, he was responsible for coordinating the implementation of the large MRCC-MSD MAPPER system described in the book. He has also been instrumental in the development of the MAPPER Report Processing System as a Sperry Univac software product. He is presently assigned to the MAPPER System Support Group of the Evaluation Programming Department of Sperry Univac, Major Systems Division, Roseville, Minnesota.